The Case of the Frightened Lady

EDGAR WALLACE

DAVIS-POYNTER

First published in this edition in 1972 by
Davis-Poynter Limited
Broadwick House Broadwick Street
London W1V 2AH

ISBN 0 7067 0043 0

Printed in Great Britain by
Lewis Reprints Limited Tonbridge Kent

CHARACTERS

MESSENGER

SERGEANT FERRABY

SERGEANT TOTTY

DETECTIVE CHIEF SUPERINTENDENT
TANNER

BRIGGS

WILMOT

LORD LEBANON

KELVER

BROOKS

GILDER

LADY LEBANON

RAWBANE

AISLA CRANE

ACT I

DETECTIVE CHIEF SUPERINTENDENT TANNER's room at
Scotland Yard. The room is set for a lecture. Up stage is a
blackboard and chalk. Down stage is a desk. There are about
16 chairs in rows for the class which is to assemble.

> (A uniformed MESSENGER enters and
> puts some letters on the desk; goes up
> stage and sees that both chalk and book
> are there. Sets a chair in its place.)
>
> (Enter SERGEANT FERRABY.)

MESSENGER: Morning, Sergeant.

FERRABY: Good morning. Is the Superintendent
about? (Goes to desk, puts report on
pad.)

MESSENGER: He's gone to a reception to these foreign
police officers who came over to London
last week.

FERRABY: Oh, of course. (Sitting at desk.) Where's
Sergeant Totty?

MESSENGER: He's somewhere in the building.

FERRABY: (Rising) I shall be in my office if I'm
wanted. You've no idea when the Superintendent is coming in?

MESSENGER: No, sir. I know he's got a prisoner to
examine.

FERRABY: All right. Tell him where I am.

> (Exit FERRABY.)
>
> (The MESSENGER opens window, arranges
> chairs, blackboard, etc.   Enter
> SERGEANT TOTTY.)
>
> Morning, Sergeant.

TOTTY: Morning.

MESSENGER:	Mr Tanner's taking the lecture this morning.
TOTTY:	So I see.
MESSENGER:	How long's he been lecturing!
TOTTY:	All his life — somebody.
MESSENGER:	I don't know, Sergeant, but I don't think police officers are any better for lectures.
TOTTY:	Did I ask you for your opinion? Did anybody ask you for your opinion?
MESSENGER:	No, Sergeant.
TOTTY:	If they do, you might tell me, will you?
MESSENGER:	Yes, Sergeant.
TOTTY:	Don't get modest about it. Come here. Tell me man to man.
MESSENGER:	Yes, Sergeant. The weather looks like clearin' up, don't it? (Cleaning the blackboard.)
TOTTY:	No. It's goin' to rain for a week.
MESSENGER:	Oh, I beg your pardon, I forgot to tell you that they've got that man over at Cannon Row when Mr Tanner's ready for him.
TOTTY:	What man?
MESSENGER:	That man from Wormwood Scrubs. He's been brought up here by a screw.
TOTTY:	(Sitting at the desk.) A screw? I don't understand thieves' slang. Do you mean a prison officer?
MESSENGER:	Yes, Sergeant.
TOTTY:	A screw' Good Gawd, what's the Service comin' to'
MESSENGER:	Well, I'm only usin' the expression——
TOTTY:	Don't use any expression — use the words accordin' to the object named. Don't let's

TOTTY: (Contd)   have any vulgarity.

MESSENGER: No, Sergeant.

(Phone rings.)

TOTTY: Screw' Nice word to use' (Goes to phone. Loudly.) All right! I know he's at Cannon Row. I know him—Coley—he used to be a tea leaf in the cut, and run around planting slush for a merchant from Peckham. I remember. All right, Coley. I'll come over for him when the bloke wants him. About ten minutes' time. I know I've got to bring the screw. All right Coley. He's got nothing to say. All he wants is a day out of stir. Mind you, they do snout sometimes, but he never had the guts for a nose. So long. (Putting down phone.) What was I sayin'?

MESSENGER: About thieves' slang, Sergeant.

TOTTY: Bear it in mind, boy.

MESSENGER: Yes, Sergeant.

(SERGEANT FERRABY enters, bringing papers.)

(Exit MESSENGER.)

TOTTY: Hullo, face!

FERRABY: Isn't Tanner back?

TOTTY: Yes—hidin' under the table.

FERRABY: (Sardonically) Ha ha!

(TOTTY is examining letters on the desk.)

TOTTY: (Reading) Mark's Priory case—Somerset House report. That's Flynn's writing. Huh! Only one 'M' in Somerset! Would you believe it in these days of education!

FERRABY:	Quite a lot of people spell it with one 'M'.
TOTTY:	Where have you been?
FERRABY:	Down to Mark's Priory for a couple of days. God, isn't that girl lovely!
TOTTY:	Which?
FERRABY:	Miss Crane. Fancy her marrying a fool like that!
TOTTY:	Who's she marrying?
FERRABY:	Lord Lebanon.
TOTTY:	Oh! Lord Lebanon. (Rising) She's a lucky girl.
FERRABY:	I've never seen a girl as depressed as she was when I spoke to her.
TOTTY:	I don't have that effect on women. You want to see them when I've done with them.
FERRABY:	If she's in love with that man I give up.
TOTTY:	It seems ridiculous she's not in love with you (Starting to draw:) don't it?
FERRABY:	Don't be a fool! What is it — a lecture?
TOTTY:	Yes. The infant class. Turnin' a copper into a busy in three lessons.
FERRABY:	How long has Tanner been taking them?
TOTTY:	Well, you know what he is? All for work, worry and wangles. What have you been doin' down at Mark's Priory? (Drawing an old man on the blackboard.)
FERRABY:	Nosing around. Checking up Briggs' statement mainly.
TOTTY:	Briggs? Oh, the lag who said he knew something about the murder.
FERRABY:	Has Tanner seen him?
TOTTY:	No. He's over at Cannon Row waiting for an audience. I can't understand

TOTTY: (Contd)	Tanner takin' any notice of what a man like that says. I've had convicts in my room confessin' to murders, never mind about throwing light on 'em, and why? So they could get brought up for a day's outing from Dartmoor! Convicts' confessions' Gawd!
FERRABY:	There's something heart-breaking about her. God, how unhappy she was'
TOTTY:	Who's this?
FERRABY:	This girl.
TOTTY:	Oh' Is that what you went down for—to cheer her up? You don't seem to have made a good job of it.
FERRABY:	Very funny' Give us a lecture, professor.
TOTTY:	(He has now drawn the picture of an old man, and begins to talk in a falsetto and refined voice.) I am taking the class to-day on the subject of nose-prints as a means of detecting crime. The portrait before you is that of Samuel Macfluter, better known as Sandy the Soak.
	(DETECTIVE CHIEF SUPERINTENDENT TANNER enters. He stands by the door watching and listening.)
	Speakin' as one of the most experienced officers at Scotland Yard——
TANNER:	Very pretty.
TOTTY:	(Looking round.) Eh?
TANNER:	Where did I meet you last—at the Police College wasn't it? Morning, Ferraby.
	(Re-enter MESSENGER with letter, which TOTTY takes from him.)
FERRABY:	Good morning, sir.
TANNER:	(To TOTTY.) Rub that out.

TOTTY: (To MESSENGER.) Rub that out, will you? And find out who did it and report him to me.

(MESSENGER rubs out picture. TANNER stands and examines letters.)

That man's at Cannon Row.

TANNER: Oh, Briggs. I want to see him. (Looking at his watch. To MESSENGER.) What time is the lecture?

MESSENGER: Eleven o'clock, sir.

TANNER: Thank you.

(MESSENGER goes towards exit.)

TOTTY: You don't want me to come to this little chat, do you?

(Exit MESSENGER.)

TANNER: Do you ever say 'sir'?

TOTTY: Yes.

TANNER: Thank God for that!

TOTTY: I'll say 'sir' if you want me to say 'sir', sir.

TANNER: (To FERRABY.) Did you get anything?

FERRABY: I only confirmed the statement, sir.

TOTTY: A waste of time.

TANNER: That's my affair. (Sitting at desk.)

TOTTY: I'm only trying to help you, boy.

TANNER: 'Sir' will do.

TOTTY: Certainly, sir.

TANNER: In the presence of subordinates it sounds good. When we are alone I will remember that we were respectively the best and the shortest policemen that ever walked a beat together.

TOTTY:	And I'm still the best.
	(TANNER is still sitting at desk reading documents.)
	Here. (Indicating FERRABY.) He's found a girl—God, how lovely she is!
TANNER:	(Looking up.) What?
FERRABY:	(To TOTTY.) Don't talk rubbish. (Turning to TANNER.) No, sir, I was telling Totty about Miss Crane.
TANNER:	(Puzzled) Miss Crane——?
FERRABY:	Lady Lebanon's niece.
TANNER:	Oh yes, oh yes, yes.
FERRABY:	She's going to be married to Lord Lebanon.
TOTTY:	It's a love match.
FERRABY:	It's nothing of the kind!
TANNER:	Well, what about her?
FERRABY:	I was only saying——
TOTTY:	God, she's so unhappy!
FERRABY:	Shut up or I'll deal with you.
TOTTY:	Wait till you're married, boy—your widow will get a pension.
FERRABY:	I met her by accident and she remembered me. (He is rather pleased about this.) Rather extraordinary—I've only been there once before.
TOTTY:	Nobody could ever forget you, boy.
TANNER:	Briggs' statement works out?
FERRABY:	Yes, sir.
TANNER:	All right. Come in after the lecture. (FERRABY turns to the door, then to TANNER.) Did you see Lord Lebanon?

FERRABY:	At a distance, yes. I didn't go up to the Priory.
TOTTY:	(To TANNER.) Do you want me?
TANNER:	Yes. You can wait.
TOTTY:	What's the good of me takin' a recruits' course? I've forgot more than anybody at Scotland Yard every knew of. If I could have passed the examination in history I'd have been Assistant Commissioner by now. Queen Elizabeth—huh!
TANNER:	I didn't know that!
TOTTY:	Well, make a note of it.
TANNER:	She wasn't a bad sort.
TOTTY:	The so-called Virgin Queen! Huh! That was a bit of a scandal, eh?
FERRABY:	The worst scandal was your saying that she died in ten-sixty-six.
TOTTY:	Does it matter when she died? Would it make me a better inspector if I knew she died in 1815? Anyway, this lecture's nothin' to do with history. I don't want to be told how criminals work. I got it there (Tapping his forehead.) That's where I got it.
FERRABY:	That's where he's got it, and it's the last place you'd look for it.
TOTTY:	I can't study and go in for athalatics, y'know.
TANNER:	Athletics?
TOTTY:	(Displaying medals on chain.) Well, I didn't get these for nothing.
TANNER:	What are they for?
TOTTY:	(Fingering medals.) Darts—Metropolitan Police Champion. That's all. Home Counties runner-up—Walthamstow Gold

TOTTY: (Contd)	Medal, more or less. Palmer's Green Open Championship — the blue ribbon of the dartin' world.
TANNER:	Astonishing'
FERRABY:	Revolting! (Exit FERRABY.)
TOTTY:	What's your typical case?
TANNER:	(Leaning back in his chair and frowning.) I don't know. I think I'll take the Mark's Priory case – it's fresh in my mind.
TOTTY:	I could tell 'em all about that — don't you think it's silly askin' me to attend a lecture like that? I <u>know.</u>
TANNER:	I'm getting in on the inside of this business.
TOTTY:	Bit in the paper about it this morning. I cut it out. (Taking cutting from pocket.) Here you are. (Reading) 'There is still no further development in the Mark's Priory mystery, though seven weeks have passed since the young chauffeur, William Studd, returning from a fancy dress ball at the village hall, was found strangled on the lawn of Mark's Priory. This is the fifteenth crime since the beginning of the year that the police has failed to solve. (Looks at TANNER.) Why don't they give some of the sergeants a chance. There's men at Scotland Yard with more brains in their little finger—'
TANNER:	What's this? Let me see. (Taking paper and scanning it.) There's nothing about sergeants here. You made that up.
TOTTY:	I tore that bit off. I didn't want to hurt anybody's feelings.
TANNER:	I asked Flynn to make a search at Somerset House — heard anything about it?

TOTTY:	(Pointing) There it is. (Sitting on desk and taking a cigarette.)
TANNER:	Are your feet working?
TOTTY:	Yes.
TANNER:	Well, use them. (TANNER opens letter and reads. Triumphantly.) That's a bit of first-class reasoning on my part!
TOTTY:	Oh, I'd like to see that.
TANNER:	I dare say you would. (Very self-satisfied.) Just an intuition!
TOTTY:	And whose! (Lighting cigarette.)
TANNER:	Mine. It came to me like a flash when I was in my bath.
TOTTY:	Funny how bright you get on Saturday nights. I've got a theory or two about this Mark's Priory case.
TANNER:	You may smoke.
TOTTY:	Thank you. I was just going to ask you. Why did the chauffeur wear Indian clothes to the dance?
TANNER:	Why was he killed at all?
TOTTY:	There was no woman in it. I chercheyed la femme, but she wasn't there.
TANNER:	He hadn't even got a girl.
TOTTY:	(Significantly) Yuh! Who found him? Dr Amersham! What was Dr Amersham doin' at two in the mornin' in the Priory Field?
TANNER:	That's what I'd like to know.
TOTTY:	Why didn't you ask me?
TANNER:	Do you know?
TOTTY:	No, but I could have easily found out. I've been making a few inquiries.
TANNER:	In your spare time?

TOTTY:	(Emphatically and impressively.) Yes. Whilst you was sleepin' at night what was I doing?
TANNER:	Drinking.
TOTTY:	Toilin' and moilin' to get the facts. Rackin' me brains gettin' here, there and everywhere after information.
TANNER:	Good gracious!
TOTTY:	The doctor's been to India!
TANNER:	Even the village policeman knows that. He went to bring back young Lord Lebanon, who had fever there.
TOTTY:	And what's more, Amersham is on the police records.
TANNER:	What? Who told you that?
TOTTY:	(Smugly) Found it myself in the files. Drivin' to the common danger — fined five pounds. Licence endorsed.
TANNER:	I see. A real hardened criminal. Has he ever sold tinned peas on Sunday? You make me sick!
TOTTY:	I wondered what it was.
TANNER:	Totty, I am worried about that case. This man Briggs, who's waiting to see me, might be able to tell me something more than he's put in his statement. Where's his dossier?
TOTTY:	He's sleepin' at Wormwood Scrubs.
TANNER:	Dossier—documents—folder.
TOTTY:	Oh! French!
TANNER:	Oh, here it is. (Taking folder from table.) Thomas Henry Briggs, alias Walters, alias Thomas, alias Smith.
TOTTY:	Yes, I know him.

TANNER:	(Reading) He's done time all over the world: India, Cape Town, Manchester. Serving the first part of his five-year sentence in Wormwood Scrubs for uttering forged notes. Central Criminal Court. July 17th. Married.
TOTTY:	What was he doing in the village?
TANNER:	He went down there to collect some notes from a snide merchant. That's how the stuff changes hands: in village pubs. They got the merchant in this case. A man named Brinsky.
TOTTY:	I know: I caught him.
TANNER:	You didn't catch him. You arrested him on a warrant. Any flat-footed copper could have done it, and you had three men with you.

(TOTTY shrugs.)

I wonder if Briggs'll tell us anything that's worth hearing?

TOTTY:	Him——no! All he wants is a joy-ride. A drive from Wormwood Scrubs to Scotland Yard is like a day excursion to him.
TANNER:	I'll see him.
TOTTY:	(Rising) Do you mind if I use your phone?
TANNER:	Is it too much trouble to walk downstairs, across the yard, into Cannon Row and bring him over?
TOTTY:	It's the dignity of the thing.
TANNER:	Be dignified on somebody else's telephone. Good Lord you're the laziest man I've ever met with'

(Exit TOTTY.)

(TANNER fills his cigarette-case.)

(Re-enter TOTTY.)

TOTTY:	He's outside. They thought I told them to bring him over.
TANNER:	That must have been a pleasant discovery for you. All right. I'll have him in.
TOTTY:	Yes. (Going to door.)
TANNER:	Totty, I am taking this examination, will you remember that?
TOTTY:	(Turning) Have I ever——
TANNER:	Yes. And smarm him a little.
TOTTY:	I have me own method.
TANNER:	Yes. Well, leave it on the mat and try mine.

(TOTTY goes to door and beckons. Enter BRIGGS — a harmless-looking man— followed by WILMOT, a prison warder.)

WILMOT:	Here's the man, sir.
TOTTY:	(Unlocking the handcuffs.) Got all your jewellery on to-day, boy? All he wants is a rope of pearls, or a rope, anyway.
BRIGGS:	That's funny, that is' You ought to be where I've been.
TOTTY:	Don't be silly — I've had my holiday.
TANNER:	(Cheerfully) Good morning, Briggs. Sit down, won't you?

(BRIGGS is about to sit in arm-chair, but TOTTY takes it from him and passes him an ordinary chair.)

TOTTY:	How is everything at the Scrubs?
BRIGGS:	I can't complain.

TANNER:	(To WILMOT.) You needn't wait, officer, unless you wish.
WILMOT:	I think I ought to, sir. He's pretty dangerous.
TOTTY:	Him—dangerous! Why——
TANNER:	(Warningly) Totty! (To WILMOT.) Is he allowed to smoke?
WILMOT:	Strictly speaking, no. But I don't suppose there'll be any complaint.
TANNER:	(To TOTTY.) Give him a cigarette.
	(TOTTY rises, puts hand in pocket, changes his mind, goes to TANNER's desk and takes a cigarette from box. WILMOT moves back and stands by the door.)
TOTTY:	Mine are good ones. Allow me to light it for you pretty. (Lighting a match.)
	(BRIGGS is looking slightly away.)
	(Gruffly) Here, you!
BRIGGS:	I beg your pardon, I'm sure. (Lighting his cigarette.) I've never been to Scotland Yard before.
TOTTY:	Come in for a cup of tea: I'm always in on Friday afternoons.
BRIGGS:	You come down and spend the week-end with us.
	(TOTTY moves to the blackboard and draws on it.)
TANNER:	(Addressing BRIGGS, evidently checking from a sheet of foolscap in his hand.) You were in the village of Mark's Priory on the night of August the eighteenth, weren't you, Briggs?

BRIGGS:	Yes, sir. That's what I made a statement about. I can't help the police the same as I'd like to help 'em. I've been put inside by perjury, believe me or believe me not, Mr Tanner. I was as innocent as a babe unborn. I've never had a ha'penny worth of slush in me possession, not till those busies searched me bag. They planted it on me to get their names in the papers. If there's a Gawd in heaven (TOTTY looks up) you'll see justice done.
TANNER:	I'm sure. Now, tell me, is there anything you want to add to this statement?
BRIGGS:	I've been thinking it over, sir, and I think it's only right that I should come forward and tell you all I know. I'm feeling faint; could I have a glass of brandy, sir?
TANNER) TOTTY)	(Together) No!
TANNER:	(Kindly) Don't try it on me, old boy.
TOTTY:	They never lose hope, do they? That's what I admire about 'em.
BRIGGS:	I was down in the village for a change of air — I've been very poorly——
TOTTY:	Tut! Tut!
BRIGGS:	——and I was stayin' at the White Hart, sir, and a gentleman called in his car. If he put counterfeit notes in me bag, sir, he put them in without me knowing. Could you ever imagine anything like it?
TOTTY:	I couldn't and you couldn't and nobody else could.
TANNER:	Now listen. I haven't brought you all the way from Wormwood Scrubs to discuss the justice of your sentence. Let's be men of the world and say you asked for it and you got it. What do you know

TANNER: (Contd)   about the Mark's Priory murder? If you
                  can't tell me anything about that, you can
                  go back.

BRIGGS: Well, sir, after this gentleman that I
                  talked about called at the White Hart, I
                  went for a stroll. It was a pretty dark
                  night and I was sittin' on the stile, smokin'
                  a pipe, when I saw a figure comin' along,
                  and it gave me a regular turn. He was
                  dressed like an Indian.

TANNER: Yes, that was the murdered man. Was he
                  alone?

BRIGGS: Yes, sir. A couple of minutes later I
                  heard a scream that made me blood
                  freeze in me marrow.

TANNER: Was it from the man in fancy dress?

BRIGGS: It came from the wood, just behind where
                  I was sitting. I got up and looked around,
                  and then I saw a man coming across the
                  field to me. He was out of breath —— a
                  gentleman of my age, with a little brown
                  beard. I shouted 'Who's there?' and he
                  said: 'That's all right. It's Dr Amersham.'

TANNER: Oh! You didn't say that in your statement.

BRIGGS: There's one or two things I didn't say in
                  me statement.

TANNER: Doctor Amersham. Well?

BRIGGS: (Impressively) Well, sir, I've got a
                  wonderful memory for voices—and
                  suddenly I remembered him.

TANNER: You'd met him before?

BRIGGS: Yes, sir. In Calcutta in the prison. Him
                  and me was waitin' trial together —— he
                  was an Army doctor, who got into trouble
                  over a kite—he signed another man's
                  name to it. Coincidence, wasn't it? I was
                  up on the same sort of charge. But he got
                  off. They squared it to save a scandal.

BRIGGS: (Contd)	Amersham, that was his name.
TANNER:	When was that?
BRIGGS:	Just sixteen years ago. That's when I got my packet.
TANNER:	Did he recognize you?
BRIGGS:	No, sir.
TANNER:	You are sure he said 'Dr Amersham'?
BRIGGS:	If I never move from this seat——
TOTTY:	What the Superintendent asked you was: are you sure it was Dr Amersham — yes or no?
TANNER:	That's all right, Sergeant. (To BRIGGS.) You can't tell me any more?
BRIGGS:	I've told you enough to get me sentence remitted, ain't I?
TANNER:	That'll do.
	(TOTTY snaps on the handcuffs.)
BRIGGS:	Excuse me, sir. You might send a note to the Home Secretary. (Rising) He only lives round the corner. A word from you would go a long way.
WILMOT:	Come on.
TANNER:	I can do nothing for you— you know that.
BRIGGS:	(Truculently) I wonder I lower meself to come to a lousy place like this. I wouldn't have if I knew as much as I know now. (Continues to talk until he exits.) Wastin' me time——and what do I get out of it? A tuppeny-ha'penny packet of fags that I wouldn't lower meself to smoke! (Ad lib.)
	(Exit BRIGGS and WILMOT.)
TOTTY:	There's gratitude!

TANNER:	What's he got to be grateful for? Do you know, Totty, I'd like to have a talk with Dr Amersham. I've had three lines to him from three different quarters and every one of them after I had made my investigations. There's a lot about that place that puzzles me. I wonder what they're after?
TOTTY:	I'll tell you what they're after. They're after Lebanon.
TANNER:	Lebanon? Yes, Amersham is. The tale that Briggs told is true. Amersham's a wrong 'un. (Taking paper from pocket.) This tells me a lot.
TOTTY:	Did you ever see the staff? The two footmen? (Rising and moving up by the blackboard.)
TANNER:	Two tough-looking fellows?
TOTTY:	Yes, they're Americans. Now why Americans? Who ever heard of an American footman? It's not natural. He'd be easy too, Viscount what's-his-name?
TANNER:	Lebanon.
TOTTY:	Young Lebanon's a mug. It would be like taking money from a child.
	(FERRABY enters hurriedly.)
FERRABY:	Excuse me, sir, will you see Lord Lebanon?
TOTTY:	Eh? That's funny.
TANNER:	Lord Lebanon? Is he here?
FERRABY:	He came to the Assistant Commissioner's office and the Assistant Commissioner asked if I'd bring him along to you.
TOTTY:	That's the bloke that's going to marry your young lady.

FERRABY: Oh, shut up!

TANNER: What does he want?

FERRABY: I don't know, sir.

TANNER: Bring him in.

(Exit FERRABY.)

TOTTY: I better stay. I've had a lot of dealings
                with the aristocracy. I know how to talk
                to 'em.

(TANNER sits.)

TANNER: I'll do the talking.

(FERRABY re-enters, followed by
LORD LEBANON.)

LORD LEBANON: Hullo! I say, am I an awful nuisance?

(Exit FERRABY.)

TOTTY: (Assuming his aristocratic voice.) Not at
                all, my lord. We are always glad to see
                visitors here. (Pushing up an arm-chair.)

LORD LEBANON: (To TANNER.) You are the fellow in
                charge of this case, aren't you, Mister
                —————?

TANNER: (Rising) My name is Tanner.

LORD LEBANON: Tanner, of course. (Looking round and
                seeing TOTTY, jerks his head signific-
                antly.) I suppose I can speak quite freely
                in front of your boy?

TANNER: Sergeant Totty.

LORD LEBANON: Totty? Very odd name, isn't it?

TOTTY: An old Italian family.

LORD LEBANON: I say, do you mind seeing if there's
                anybody outside that door?

TANNER:	People don't listen at doors at Scotland Yard.
LORD LEBANON:	Really? How do you find things out? I suppose people tell you?
TOTTY:	(In his aristocratic voice.) We have a system of intelligence here ——
TANNER:	Are you used to people listening at your doors, Lord Lebanon?
LORD LEBANON:	Well—er—it's very awkward and I hardly know what to say. In fact, I only made up my mind last night that I'd come along and see you. We have met, haven't we?
TANNER:	Yes. I met you when I was at Mark's Priory.
LORD LEBANON:	I seem to remember your boy too.
TANNER:	Sergeant Totty.
LORD LEBANON:	Oh, I beg your pardon. The old Italian family —— yes. Devilish odd for Italians to be at Scotland Yard. I suppose you get all sorts of people here. I don't know much about Italians.
TOTTY:	We haven't been Italian for quite a number of years.
LORD LEBANON:	Has he got something the matter with his voice?
TANNER:	No, no, just a touch of croup. You made up your mind to come and see me last night. Won't you sit down?
LORD LEBANON:	Thank you. (Sitting) I know very little about Scotland Yard, except that it's a place where you keep prisoners.
	(TOTTY takes LORD LEBANON's hat, gloves and umbrella, and puts them on a chair.)
	By the way, who was that fellow who showed me in?

TANNER:	Sergeant Ferraby.
LORD LEBANON:	Really? A detective —— is he really? Good Lord! I thought he was a gentleman.
TANNER:	Very likely he is.
TOTTY:	Yes, there are many old Etonians heah. May I say ——
TANNER:	No. Will you go on, Lord Lebanon?
LORD LEBANON:	The whole thing is very vulgar, and when one's mother is in it, you know — Good Lord! that sort of gets you... Everything was all right while my dear old father was alive. Shocking invalid! He never left his room for fifteen years. Perfectly ghastly! When I went out to India everything was quite charming and agreeable. You know what it is—one had an awful lot of fun.
TOTTY:	Yes, yes.
LORD LEBANON:	People were most pleasant. When my dear old father died, perhaps I ought to have come back, but I stayed on till I got my fever and Amersham came over and said: 'You'd better go home.' I didn't want to go home —— you know how it is?
TOTTY:	Quate.
LORD LEBANON:	But I thought I'd better get back and do something serious. Take my seat in the House. Not that I approve of the House of Lords. I'm rather a democrat.
TANNER:	So you came back. Were things changed at all?
LORD LEBANON:	Oh, devilishly. Almost everything was changed —— my mother, and my—— er— Miss Crane. You've met Miss Crane?
TANNER:	Miss Crane? Oh, yes; that was the pretty young lady who was staying at the Priory when I was there—you called her——

TOTTY: Alice.

TANNER:)
LORD LEBANON:) Aisla!

LORD LEBANON: She's a sort of cousin, you know, and
she's lived with us for years. Her
people are desperately poor. My mother
has always made her a sort of allowance.
Quite a nice girl. But I've got to marry
her and that's very awkward.

TOTTY: Ah, yes. We've had similar cases in our
family.

TANNER: What do you mean, Lord Lebanon? You've
<u>got</u> to marry her? You're in love with the
young lady?

LORD LEBANON: No, that's the poisonous part of it; I'm
not. I'm not in love with anybody. I'll
tell you in the strictest confidence. I'm
sure your boy here — (Pointing to
TOTTY.)

TANNER: You can rely on Sergeant Totty.

LORD LEBANON: I don't love her. She's a terribly nice
girl, but—er—something odd about her.
Since that infernal murder she's frightened.

TANNER: Oh?

LORD LEBANON: My dear fellow, she walks in her sleep!
I've seen her. I mean, it's awfully
disconcerting, one is sitting up, having
a whisky and soda, and one sees a girl in
her nightdress walking down the stairs...
I mean, it's terrifying!

TANNER: You say she's frightened. Of what?

LORD LEBANON: I don't know. Just frightened of everything — jumps when you speak to her. I
wouldn't be a bit surprised if it isn't these
two fellows that my mother has in the
house.

TANNER: Oh! (He and TOTTY exchange glances.)

TANNER: (Contd) The footmen?

LORD LEBANON: Footmen! (Laughing) I've never seen footmen like them. They're simply impossible. Upon my word, I'm not exaggerating — if you tell them to pour out a drink they slop it over the tray. They talk to my mother as though she were a servant and they were the masters of the house! If I go out of my room in the night — I don't sleep very well since my fever — I find them loafing about the corridor. I mean, it's getting intolerable, really!

TANNER: Why don't you discharge them?

LORD LEBANON: Discharge them! But I do! Six days a week, but they're still there. I've never known anything like it — and I don't suppose anybody else has either.

TANNER: But you are the master — let me put it vulgarly — you are the boss?

LORD LEBANON: Oh, I'm the boss, in a way, but when a fellow's got a mother — but perhaps it's not so easy for you to understand the position. It's a very difficult situation. I'm a thinker, not a man of action. I don't want any bother or fuss. Anything for peace and quietness. I did kick about marrying somebody I didn't want to marry, but I suppose it doesn't matter who you marry, though I must confess I'm not terribly keen on marrying a girl who walks in her sleep. I mean, one can't go running all over the house to find one's wife in the middle of the night!

TOTTY: (In his natural voice.) What about this Dr Amersham?

LORD LEBANON: (Starting) You've got your voice back? Well, you might as well know that Dr Amersham is a man I dislike intensely.

LORD LEBANON: (Contd)	Perhaps I oughtn't to say that, but we're all friends here, aren't we?
TANNER:	Is he a friend of her ladyship?
LORD LEBANON:	Well, I suppose he is. He's a nasty fellow. He doesn't like me, and he doesn't like Aisla, and he doesn't like anybody. Upon my word, the only people he gets on with are the footmen. I saw them hobnobbing when they didn't know I was watching them the morning before that poor chauffeur fellow was killed. Perfectly ghastly affair! Made me ill for a week.
TANNER:	Are you afraid of these men?
LORD LEBANON:	(Smiling) Well, I don't know about being afraid. It's terribly upsetting. You can't get away from them — listening and prying. (Looking round.) I say (To TOTTY) do you mind seeing if there's anybody outside the door.
TOTTY:	(Shaking his head.) There's nobody there.
LORD LEBANON:	Just to oblige me.
TANNER:	Sergeant.
	(TOTTY goes to door and opens it. GILDER, the footman, is standing there. LORD LEBANON comes to his feet.)
TOTTY:	What do you want?
	(TANNER rises.)
GILDER:	(Suavely) His lordship left home without his cigarette-case. I thought I'd bring it to him.
LORD LEBANON:	Who told you to follow me?
GILDER:	I only saw you by accident coming into this place.

25

TANNER: Why were you standing at the door
                  listening? Who allowed you to come up?

GILDER: I asked a policeman which was Mr
                  Tanner's room and he told me. (To LORD
                  LEBANON.) Your lordship's case. (Cross-
                  ing and handing him case.) Excuse me,
                  gentlemen. (Goes to door and exits.)

TANNER: (To TOTTY.) Follow that man down the
                  stairs. See where he goes. (To LORD
                  LEBANON.) What's his name?

                  (Exit TOTTY.)

LORD LEBANON: That's Gilder. (Sitting again.) You see?

TANNER: Has that happened to you before?

LORD LEBANON: My dear fellow, I thought one day I'd
                  left them well behind me in the country
                  and when I turned round I found them both
                  following me in Bond Street. It's rather
                  exasperating! One doesn't want to make
                  an exhibition of oneself in a public street,
                  but for two pins I'd have given them both
                  a good thrashing!

TANNER: (Crossing to him.) Why have you come to
                  me now?

LORD LEBANON: Well, I'll be perfectly frank with you. I
                  don't want to make a fool of myself. I
                  mean, I don't want to make a scene. At
                  the same time I don't want to die
                  particularly.

TANNER: It's like that? Aren't you possibly
                  exaggerating?

LORD LEBANON: I don't know whether I am or whether I'm
                  not. All I know is that I don't understand
                  what's going on.

TANNER: Do you think there' some chance of your
                  being killed? Who's the heir to your
                  property?

26

LORD LEBANON: Oh, some cousin in America. He's a
waiter or a servant of some sort. Isn't
it ridiculous!

TANNER: You're very rich, aren't you?

LORD LEBANON: Oh, yes; the taxation is perfectly ghastly,
but I've got plenty of money.

TANNER: What are you afraid of?

LORD LEBANON: I know it sounds like one of those
ridiculous stories that one reads in
sensational books, but honestly, I mean —
I think there's something particularly odd
going on, if you understand me, and that
these two fellows are, not to put too fine
a point on it, employed by——

TANNER: Your mother?

LORD LEBANON: I don't know. I really don't know what to
think. There are these two men, there's
Amersham, who does as he damned well
likes in my house — comes and goes
when he likes. There's this wretched girl
who's always frightened, and I'm sort of
engaged to her. It's an awful mess-up.
Honestly, I wish you'd come down and put
it right. I mean, if it's a matter of money,
I'd spare no expense——

TANNER: (Shaking his head and smiling.) I'm afraid
we can't undertake that kind of job at
Scotland Yard, but I'm most anxious to
know something more about Amersham.
He's got a place in London. I believe I'm
right in saying he's retired?

LORD LEBANON: I wish he'd retire from my house. Yes,
he is. (Rising) And I'll tell you something
you don't know. When he was in India a
woman was killed — in his bungalow.
Indian woman... beautiful girl...
strangled.

TANNER: That's news to me.

27

LORD LEBANON: Strangled with a sort of cloth. Naturally
there was a terrible row about it. A
very good-class girl. I mean, it wasn't
as though it was somebody common. She
was quite well-connected.

TANNER: Can you give me particulars?

LORD LEBANON: You come down and see me and I'll tell
you everything about it. But I don't want
you to tell him I told you. I mean, I don't
want any quarrel with the man.

(Enter TOTTY.)

TANNER: I'll be going to Mark's Priory at the end
of this week.

LORD LEBANON: And I say, you won't breathe a word to
my mother, will you? It's perfectly awful
of me to talk about her the way I have,
but possibly she's as much under Amersham's thumb as I am.

(TANNER motions to TOTTY to give LORD
LEBANON his hat. TOTTY gets hat,
gloves and umbrella, goes and opens the
door.)

TANNER: Lord Lebanon, I think you still know
something about Dr Amersham that you
haven't told me.

LORD LEBANON: I do know quite a lot.

TANNER: What is it?

LORD LEBANON: (Pulling on his gloves slowly as he walks
towards door. Turning to TANNER.)
Come down to Mark's Priory and perhaps
I'll tell you. So sorry to have bothered
you. Oh, I beg your pardon. (Coming
back from the door and shaking hands
with TANNER.) Good-bye, Mr Tanner.
Good-bye, Mr— I never can remember
foreign names. I hope you'll come to the

LORD LEBANON: (Contd)	Priory and I hope I shall be alive to see you. (Exit)
TOTTY:	Forty thousand a year! I'd like to change places with him!
TANNER:	I've got an idea you would be very unlucky if you did. (Picking up house phone.) Records. Seven.
TOTTY:	If the boys ever find him he'll be their old-age pension. I wonder if he plays cards?
TANNER:	(At the phone.) Is that you, Alec? Have you any record at all of Dr Leicester Charles Amersham? No, you won't find him on the home list, but you may have him in the Indian records. If you find anything, will you send it down? Thank you. (Replacing the receiver.)
TOTTY:	I've been right through the records. What's the good of tryin' to improve on me?
	(FERRABY enters.)
	If I missed anything, the man who finds it is entitled to a gold medal. Are you going down to Mark's Priory?
TANNER:	Yes.
TOTTY:	I might come along with you.
TANNER:	I daresay you might if you're asked.
TOTTY:	It's no good taking a new man when you've got somebody who knows the case backwards. Mind you, I don't mind being done out of a bit of credit. It's happened before, and it'll happen again. I've done the work and the other man has got the promotion. If I'd known when Queen Elizabeth died—
FERRABY:	I'd like to go down, Mr Tanner.
TANNER:	(With a smile.) I can't have the whole of Scotland Yard down there to make an

29

TANNER: (Contd) inquiry about Dr Amersham.

FERRABY: I've spoken to this girl, and I had a feeling that once or twice she was on the point of telling me something.

TANNER: If she has anything to tell, why doesn't she tell her fiancé?

TOTTY: Have you seen him?

FERRABY: I don't think he's the kind of man she could tell — he's under his mother's influence. Why, that's the talk of the village.

TOTTY: If you turned that girl over to me for half an hour — only half an hour —

TANNER: It would seem like eternity to her. Yes, if I go you can come along.

FERRABY: Thank you, sir.

TOTTY: You keep your mind off women.

TANNER: Oh, dry up. (Rising and looking at watch.) Totty, when was it he said that girl got frightened?

TOTTY: After the murder.

FERRABY: She wasn't frightened when we were there.

TOTTY: She hadn't seen much of you then.

TANNER: Miss Crane? Yes, I remember her. (To TOTTY.) All right, bring them in. (He takes a red cloth in tissue paper from the drawer at up-stage end of desk, and puts it in the basket on the desk.)

(Exit FERRABY.)

(TOTTY goes, calls the MEN and enters again. The MEN file in.)

TOTTY: (With list.) Don't make a noise. No smoking and no talking, and not so much

30

TOTTY: (Contd)   of the shurrup. File into the front seats, and when the front seats are occupied take the next seats, and so on ad nauseam.

(The MEN do so.)

Answer your names. (He calls them out one by one from his list and the MEN answer. Turning to TANNER.) Present and correct sir. Do you want me to stay? I've done the work.

TANNER: Sit down and try to learn something.

TOTTY: Yes, sir, if there's anything to learn I'll learn it, sir. ha, ha!

TANNER: And you can take them through the routine.

TOTTY: O.K., chief. (Sits in arm-chair.)

TANNER: Not so much of the 'O.K., chief.' I must apologize to you men for again inflicting myself on you as a lecturer. In the absence of Superintendent Jarvis there is nothing else I can do. If anybody tells you I like lecturing, you can call him a liar. I spoke to you last Wednesday about detective work on broad lines. Any of you men who have come from the uniformed branch with the illusion that you are going to have an easy time, had better get the idea out of your heads. And any of you fellows who have been reading thrillers and think you are going to have a romantic time can forget it. The really interesting detective work never goes on outside of the magazine.

TOTTY: Which magazine?

TANNER: It doesn't matter which magazine— any magazine. That is where the real detectives live. They aren't detectives as much as scientists. The moment they meet you they can tell you all you know about yourself and a little bit more. The only thing an

31

TANNER: (Contd) ordinary detective can tell you from mud-stains is that somebody has been in the mud — and any damn' fool knows that. He may deduce or he may deduct, as the case may be, but the safest plan is to be tipped off by somebody who knows. It is a waste of time spending your nights sitting in your beautiful studies or libraries, examining hairs through microscopes to discover who the criminal is if you can go round to the 'Bull and Dog' and find a man who can tell you his name and address for a pound. While I am drawing a sketch to illustrate my typical case I will ask that distinguished orator Sergeant Totty to explain the duties of a detective officer when he is called in to a case of homicide. (Moving up to back of blackboard and drawing.)

TOTTY: (To the blackboard.) Homicide is not one of the peculiar habits of the criminal classes, but as a rule the recreation or amusement of amateurs who want to get on in the world, such as labourers, lawyers, insurance agents and stockbrokers.

TANNER: Keep to facts.

TOTTY: If you are called in to a case of murder or homicide your first duty is to inform your divisional commander and a Detective Chief Superintendent, accompanied by a capable sergeant, will be on the spot in a few minutes and will take all the credit that is going, the sergeant or subordinate doing the work.

TANNER: Keep to facts.

TOTTY: You will allow no unauthorized person to enter the house or apartment. You will not move or attempt to touch the late deceased until the divisional police surgeon comes along and gives you the all right, or O.K. (Turning to a policeman.)

TOTTY: (Contd)	What are you eating?
POLICEMAN:	Chocolates, sir.
TOTTY:) TANNER:)	Good God!

(TOTTY takes paper bag from policeman and puts them in his pocket.)

TOTTY: (Pausing) You will keep your hands away from any shiny surface: plate, knives, table-tops, money, whiskey-bottles, filled or unfilled, anything that can hold finger-prints. Search the apartment or house for any article of clothing that may have been left behind by the murderer. Feel the towels in the bathroom, whether they are wet or dry. See if there is any sign of the murderer having washed his hands, face, or any other portion of his anatomy.

(One of the policemen laughs, puts hand to mouth, and gets a look from TOTTY.)

Search the floor carefully for anything that might have been dropped. If any article of furniture has been overturned or disturbed, it should be left until the arrival of the Superintendent and the capable sergeant, who will tell him what to do. (Looks at TANNER.)

TANNER: That's more than enough, Totty. Thank you. (He moves up to the blackboard.)

(TOTTY crosses to chair, sits. Policemen clap.)

Stop that! To-day I'm going to give you a typical case of the unsolved mystery of Mark's Priory. I use the newspaper expression 'unsolved mystery' because you will probably recognize it better than the official description which is 'unfinished case.' Make a note of this — 'unfinished

33

TANNER: (Contd)   case.' Mark's Priory is a little village in Sussex. It is about five miles from the nearest railway station and is the seat of Lord Lebanon — The Lebanons are a very old family who settled in England after the Wars of the Crusaders. This is the establishment. (Pointing to diagram on blackboard.) East wing, west wing, and this is the main hall. Here is a broad drive, stretching down to what is known as Priory Field, a meadow of about sixty acres. Here, on the right, is a belt of trees which runs up parallel with the side of the house and spreads out behind into what is known as Mark's Priory Park. The household when I made my visit consisted of Lady Lebanon (Pointing to names as he mentions them.) Lord Lebanon, her son, who had recently got home from India; Miss Aisla Crane, her ladyship's niece and secretary; a butler named Kelver; two footmen, whose names I don't know — yes, one of them is Gilder— two cooks, a few maids and the like. (To TOTTY.) Are you listening, Totty?

TOTTY: (Waking up.) Eh? Yes, sir, I was listening.

TANNER: What did I say?

TOTTY: I couldn't say it as well as you, sir.

TANNER: There was, in addition, before I arrived, a man named William Studd, a chauffeur, single, highly respectable young man with apparently no enemies. To these must be added a Dr Amersham. Now, for reasons which I cannot understand — and if I can't nobody else can——

(TOTTY coughs.)

That's a very bad cough of yours, Totty. Perhaps you'd like to go outside and get a drink of water? For reasons which, as I said, nobody understood or understands,

34

TANNER: (Contd)   Dr Amersham is permitted access to the house day and night.

TOTTY: Here, you never told me this.

TANNER: Strange! On the night of August the eighteenth there was a fancy-dress ball at the village hall on behalf of the village bowling club. Studd, the chauffeur, and three other members of the staff attended that ball dressed in home-made costumes. Studd chose that of an Indian. He left the hall rather late and was seen by the village constable and by a man whom I interviewed this morning, just before he went into the field. He was found the next morning — (Picking up a piece of blue cloth.) strangled with this. This is a piece of cloth of Indian manufacture. (Throwing it at the class. They dodge it.) Notice the little metal tag in the corner — the trade-mark of the maker. Look at it.

TOTTY: Go on—it won't bite you.

TANNER: The body was found between two groups of rhododendrons that grew somewhere about here (making a cross on board) and had evidently been dragged there by the murderer. Now the only other person in the field that night, and why he was there nobody knows, but I am going to find out, was Dr Amersham. Dr Amersham, when questioned by me at the time ———

(The MESSENGER enters.)

MESSENGER: Urgent minute, sir!

TANNER: (Quickly) Take it, Totty.

(TOTTY goes to MESSENGER and takes the message, opens the envelope, reads it. Exit MESSENGER.)

As I said, Dr Amersham stated at the time that he had not left his bed that night,

35

TANNER: (Contd)   and that he was nowhere near the place. That was not true. Now, I don't mind telling you that Dr Amersham is under suspicion.

TOTTY: (Starting up from his chair, looking at the message.) Excuse me, sir, did you say the body was found near the west wing?

TANNER: (Pointing to the plan.) Yes.

TOTTY: Near some bushes eighty yards south of the west wing?

TANNER: (Pointing to the cross near the bushes.) Yes.

(TOTTY crosses to the board, looking first at the message and then at the cross.)

TOTTY: That's where they found the body of Dr Amersham half an hour ago — strangled!

QUICK CURTAIN

36

ACT II

Scene 1

The SCENE is the Prior's Hall at Mark's Priory. A very beautiful room. There are three arches in the back wall.

(When the CURTAIN rises, KELVER, the butler, TANNER, TOTTY, FERRABY, BROOKS and GILDER, are discovered.)

TANNER: What room is this?

KELVER: This is the lounge, sir. It was originally the entrance hall, or, as they called it, the Prior's Hall, but some years ago, the late Lord Lebanon had it converted.

TANNER: I see. A sort of common room?

TOTTY: (Looking round.) Nothing common about it—a bit 'ighbrow I should call it.

               (TANNER looks sharply at him.)

KELVER: Well, yes, sir. Her ladyship sometimes works here.

TOTTY: A workroom. (Seeing TANNER's glance.) No?

TANNER: You're Gilder?

GILDER: (Very suave.) Yes, sir.

TANNER: How long have you been here?

GILDER: Eight years.

TANNER: You were here in the days of the late Lord Lebanon? (Beckons to GILDER, who crosses to him.)

GILDER: Yes, sir. (He is smiling as he talks.)

TANNER: A footman?

GILDER:	Yes, Sir.
TANNER:	(Consulting notes.) Got an account at the London and Provincial Bank, haven't you?
GILDER:	Clever of you to find out. Yes, I have.
TANNER:	Unusual, isn't it, for a footman to have an account at a London bank?
GILDER:	Some of us are thrifty.
TANNER:	A pretty substantial balance, I hope?
GILDER:	(Still smiling.) Three or four thousand pounds. I've speculated wisely.
TANNER:	What is your salary here?
GILDER:	Quite a good one.
TANNER:	All right. (To BROOKS.) Your name is Brooks?
BROOKS:	Yuh. (Goes to GILDER.)
TANNER:	An American citizen, too?
BROOKS:	Yuh. But no banking account. Some of us American citizens have lost a lot of money lately.
TANNER:	You've been here very long?
BROOKS:	Six years.
TANNER:	And a footman?
BROOKS:	Sure.
TANNER:	Why is a man like you in service?
BROOKS:	(With a smile.) Well, I guess I'm naturally servile.
TANNER:	What's that scar on your face?
BROOKS:	That—— why, I got that way back in a rough house.
TANNER:	Were you a footman then?
BROOKS:	I guess I was.
TANNER:	I'd like to talk to you later.

BROOKS:	Sure.
GILDER:	Does that apply to me too, Captain?
TANNER:	No. Do you know this house very well?
GILDER:	Every inch of it.
TANNER:	Lady Lebanon said I might see over it. Perhaps you could show me round.
GILDER:	Yes—if I can spare the time—— (GILDER bows and exits. BROOKS follows him at leisure.)
TOTTY:	If they're footmen. I'm a film star.
TANNER:	(To KELVER.) What do they do?
KELVER:	(With a shrug.) They wait on her ladyship, on his lordship and on Miss Crane.
TANNER:	Where is she? Is that the lady I saw on the lawn? Ask her if she'd mind seeing me, will you, Ferraby?
FERRABY:	Yes, sir. (Exit FERRABY.)
TANNER:	(To KELVER.) You heard nothing last night?
KELVER:	No, sir.
TANNER:	No scream or shout or anything?
KELVER:	No, sir.
TANNER:	You remember the night the chauffeur, Studd, was killed?
KELVER:	Yes, sir, I remember it.
TANNER:	You heard nothing then?
KELVER:	No, sir, if you remember (TANNER moves to the desk.) I told you when you were here at the time. (TANNER opens the drawer of the desk.) That's her ladyship's desk.
TANNER:	I know. To your knowledge were there any visitors here—in this room— last night?

39

KELVER: No, sir.

TANNER: None of the domestic staff for instance, told you about somebody calling quite late?

KELVER: No, sir. Pardon me, sir. I thought I saw you speaking to her ladyship's maid, Celia Clark.

TANNER: Yes, I was.

KELVER: She was discharged this morning. Possibly she might tell you — she has had access to this part of the house.

TANNER: Yes, I've seen her. Just wait, will you? (Crossing to TOTTY.) This man may know something. Have a talk with him. Not immediately. Drop in on him when he's alone and be a little discreet.

TOTTY: Trust me!

TANNER: I don't.

TOTTY: Thanks.

(LADY LEBANON enters, carrying a portfolio.)

LADY LEBANON: Have you all you require, Mr Tanner?

TANNER: Thank you. I think you've met my assistant — Sergeant Totty?

(LADY LEBANON glances at TOTTY, then puts the portfolio on the desk.)

TOTTY: Sergeant Totty. Acting Inspector. (TANNER looks at him.) Sergeant Totty.

LADY LEBANON: Will you finish your inquiries to-day?

TANNER: I don't think so.

LADY LEBANON: I have ordered rooms for you at the White Hart.

TANNER: Thank you. I had already ordered the rooms. You told me I might look over

40

TANNER: (Contd)   the house.

LADY LEBANON: Of course. Brooks will show you round. (Touching the bell on the desk.) But the man seems to have been killed in the park.

TANNER: (With a frown.) The man?

LADY LEBANON: Dr Amersham.

TANNER: Yes, he was killed in the park; this house is in the park. It is quite possible some-body may have heard—well, sounds.

LADY LEBANON: (Sitting down at the desk, opening the portfolio and turning the loose leaves idly.) That would be interesting to find out.

TANNER: Very! (Turning to TOTTY.)

(BROOKS enters.)

LADY LEBANON: Kelver! Has anybody called?

KELVER: M'lady, Mr Rawbane is here, but I told him that in the circumstances I thought you wouldn't see him to-day.

LADY LEBANON: Show him in, please.

KELVER: Yes, my lady. (Exit)

LADY LEBANON: Brooks, show Mr Tanner over the house.

BROOKS: Sure, my lady.

TANNER: Sergeant! (To LADY LEBANON.) You'll excuse me?

(As TANNER, TOTTY and BROOKS exit, BROOKS and LADY LEBANON exchange glances. BROOKS nods. LADY LEBANON opens a drawer of the desk and takes out red cloth, similar to that seen in Act I. She goes swiftly to a stove and drops the cloth in. She closes the opening, goes back to the desk and shuts the drawer.)

41

(KELVER enters with MR RAWBANE who carries a portfolio under his arm. He is a man of some dignity, more than a workman, less than an artist.)

LADY LEBANON: Good afternoon, Mr Rawbane, I asked you to see me at five o'clock. It is now twenty past. Thank you, Kelver.

(Exit KELVER.)

RAWBANE: I thought perhaps you would rather the matter stood over for a day or two. It was a great shock to me—this dreadful affair.

LADY LEBANON: Mr Rawbane, there are dreadful affairs happening somewhere every day, but we have to live our lives and attend to our business.

RAWBANE: Naturally—er—Lady Lebanon.

(LADY LEBANON opens the portfolio.)

But I thought that you wouldn't want to be bothered with the question of redecorating the hall and so—er——

LADY LEBANON: These designs are very satisfactory, but you've made several really glaring mistakes.

RAWBANE: (Overlooking her.) I'm sorry.

LADY LEBANON: I thought you were an authority on the matter of blazonry?

RAWBANE: Well, the College of Heralds consults me occasionally.

LADY LEBANON: (Pointing) This is entirely wrong.

RAWBANE: That is the coat of the seventh Baron.

LADY LEBANON: Three water budgets on a field azure and a stag at gaze. My dear Mr Rawbane, they were never in the Lebanon quarterings!

42

RAWBANE: No? I thought they were brought into the family by Anne of Clovely.

LADY LEBANON: No, no, no! Anne brought in on a field gules party per fess dancette charged with three cinquefoils. I'll put my pencil through that.

RAWBANE: I can't understand how I made the mistak

LADY LEBANON: (Turning over leaves.) And here—on a field Goutte de Sang. But you've got this entirely wrong! Geoffrey de Ghent, who married the sister of Henry Lebanon and was, therefore, the grandfather of the tenth Baron, marshalled his arms counter-quartered—you have made them quarterly of six. That's rather a dreadful mistake, you know.

RAWBANE: I suppose it is, Lady Lebanon, but honestly I can't think of anything to say. The last time I was here poor Dr Amersham——It doesn't bear thinking of——

LADY LEBANON: In several cases you have drawn mullets where there should have been estoile.

RAWBANE: I can't give you my attention, my lady, I really can't. Why, it only seems yesterday that he was talking to me— I was explaining this very matter, that an estoile and a mullet were two different kinds of stars——

LADY LEBANON: Mr Rawbane, I am not asking you to discuss Dr Amersham. It is very sad, and we are all dreadfully sorry. His death was not important compared with eternity. These arms are part of eternity. An unbroken line for twelve hundred years. John Sieur de Toine was knighted John of Lebanon by Richard Plantagenet before Jerusalem, and it was an old family even then.

RAWBANE: If your ladyship will permit me, I can admire your detachment, that in the

43

RAWBANE: midst of all these dreadful happenings you
(Contd)   can keep your mind on the family.

LADY LEBANON: (Handing back the portfolio.) Before you
               make your models, you will correct these,
               won't you, Mr Rawbane? (Ringing bell.)

               (KELVER enters.)

               (Exit MR RAWBANE, KELVER is
               following.)

               Kelver.

KELVER: Yes, my lady.

LADY LEBANON: When are those detectives going?

KELVER: I get the impression they won't be
               leaving for quite a while.

LADY LEBANON: Where is Miss Crane?

KELVER: She was on the lawn. One of the gentlemen
               went out to bring her in.

LADY LEBANON: (Sharply) One of the police officers?

KELVER: Yes, my lady. The young-looking gentle-
               man.

LADY LEBANON: Ask her to be good enough to come to me.

KELVER: Yes, my'lady. If your ladyship will pardon
               me, I did wish to speak to you on rather
               an unpleasant matter—(Quickly) unpleas-
               ant for me, that is to say. To-morrow is
               the end of the month and I would like your
               ladyship, with all due respect, to accept
               my notice from that day.

LADY LEBANON: Your notice?

KELVER: Your ladyship is aware of the very
               distressing happenings—sensational—if
               I may call them so, that have brought us
               a great deal of undesirable publicity.

LADY LEBANON: That is hardly an affair of yours, Kelver.

44

KELVER: Pardon me, my lady. I realize that it is very disagreeable for your ladyship and his lordship, but it also has a detrimental effect upon myself. In all my years of service I have never had my name associated with matters which were——your ladyship will pardon me if I describe them as being of vulgar public interest.

LADY LEBANON: In what way do these affairs affect you, Kelver?

KELVER: Ladies and gentlemen, m'lady, shrink from contact with matters which have been the subject of public discussion and they look askance at an upper servant who has figured even indirectly in——(Finds it difficult to say.)——a police case——a murder case——two murder cases, m'lady. I have to be worthy of my past. Your ladyship will remember that I had the honour for many years to be the butler of his Serene Highness the Duke of Mekenstein and Zieburg, and that I was for many years with His Grace the Duke of Colnbrook.

LADY LEBANON: Very well. You would like to leave at the end of next month?

KELVER: If your ladyship pleases.

LADY LEBANON: I suppose the—men have something to do with it—Brooks and Gilder?

KELVER: I am almost reconciled, or, shall I say, hardened—calloused would perhaps be the better word—to these two persons.

LADY LEBANON: If they're rude to you——

KELVER: Oh, I assure your ladyship that they have always been most polite and, with the limited means at their disposal, obliging. In all my experience of service I have never known their parallel, but I am willing to recognize, my lady, the social

45

KELVER
(Contd)
upheavals of today, and I assure your ladyship that I have no criticism to offer.

LADY LEBANON: Very well, Kelver.

(Enter LORD LEBANON. Sees LADY LEBANON and is about to make a hasty retreat, but she stops him.)

Willie, I want to see you, please.

LORD LEBANON: I was just going down to the village.

(Enter GILDER.)

LADY LEBANON: That can wait. Do you want me, Gilder?

GILDER: No, my lady. I was looking for Brooks. (Exit Gilder.)

LORD LEBANON: It's like his infernal cheek——

LADY LEBANON: Willie! (To KELVER.) Thank you, Kelver.

(Exit KELVER.)

LORD LEBANON: Really, Mother, I'm not going to stand this much longer. Gilder has been following me about, and every time I tried to speak to the policeman fellow——

LADY LEBANON: There's no necessity for you to speak to policemen. Why did you go to London this morning?

LORD LEBANON: Because I damned well wanted to go!

LADY LEBANON: Willie!

LORD LEBANON: Sorry, Mother, but really, Mother, you treat me as if I were a baby.

LADY LEBANON: You went to Scotland Yard. That was very tiresome of you. Why did you go to Scotland Yard?

LORD LEBANON: (Sulkily) There are things happening in this place that are getting on my nerves. I mean, I'm not a child ——

LADY LEBANON: If there is anything the police should know you may be sure they will know it without your help. It was extra-ordinarily vulgar of you and you hurt me very much. As for Dr Amersham——

LORD LEBANON: I say, what do you think about that?

LADY LEBANON: I'm not going to discuss it with you. (Quickly) Did you tell the police anything about him?

LORD LEBANON: No. I told them he was strange and that I didn't understand him and I told them there was a lot of things I didn't understand in this house. I don't understand Gilder. I don't understand Brooks. Good Lord, they're the most extraordinary fellows——(She looks at him and he stops.)

LADY LEBANON: Willie, are we to have that again?

LORD LEBANON: I wish to God I'd never come back from India!

LADY LEBANON: Willie! You will not go to London again unless you ask me, and you are not to speak to the police about anything that happens in this house. You understand?

LORD LEBANON: (Doggedly) Yes, Mother.

LADY LEBANON: I would like you to conduct yourself with a little more dignity. Policemen and people of that sort are not the kind of men that the nineteenth Viscount Lebanon can make friends of.

LORD LEBANON: (Sullenly) I don't know. They're as good as I am. All this family nonsense... You know that fellow Gilder came up to Scotland Yard?

LADY LEBANON: He did it on my instructions. Is that sufficient?

LORD LEBANON: Yes, Mother.

LADY LEBANON: Where is Aisla?

47

LORD LEBANON: I saw her outside. She was talking to one of those fellows.

LADY LEBANON: (Sharply) Which fellows?

LORD LEBANON: One of those detective fellows. As a matter of fact, I saw him at Scotland Yard this morning. He talks like a gentleman. I suppose they pick it up.

LADY LEBANON: Willie, here are some cheques to sign.

LORD LEBANON: Blanks again?

LADY LEBANON: (Handing him a pen.) I'll fill them up.

(LORD LEBANON sits in front of the desk.)

LORD LEBANON: But, Mother, isn't it rather stupid. You never give me a cheque to sign with any figures on it. I do feel I ought to know something about——

LADY LEBANON: Sign four. They will be sufficient. And please be careful not to blot them.

(LORD LEBANON signs the cheques.)

LORD LEBANON: One, two, three, four. Mother, I don't know anything about business, but this is a terribly dangerous method.

(Enter KELVER.)

What are these for?

LADY LEBANON: (Picking up the cheque-book.) Thank you. (To KELVER.) Did you find Miss Crane?

KELVER: Yes, my lady, but she was talking rather confidentially to a gentleman and I didn't like to interrupt her.

LADY LEBANON: Tell Miss Crane, I wish to see her at once, please, whether she is talking or not.

KELVER: Yes, my lady. (Exit KELVER.)

48

LORD LEBANON: Mother, what are we going to do about Aisla? (Looking round.) It's rather important. I mean, she's terribly nice, but—er——

LADY LEBANON: I don't wish to discuss Aisla.

(LORD LEBANON is fiddling with the phone.)

Put that down and don't fiddle!

LORD LEBANON: You don't want to discuss her, but, damn it! you want me to marry her, don't you? (She looks at him.) Sorry. I should have thought I was entitled to discuss her however odd she is.

LADY LEBANON: Odd? What do you mean?

LORD LEBANON: Of course, she's awfully sweet, and agreeable, and all that, and she is a sort of relation, but I'm not in love with her— that's the truth.

LADY LEBANON: What did you mean by 'odd'?

LORD LEBANON: Well, she is odd. I mean, she wanders about the house walking in her sleep, she's frightened of her own shadow, jumps when you talk to her——

LADY LEBANON: Naturally. She's very highly strung.

LORD LEBANON: (Doggedly—looking at his finger-nails.) Well, I think she's a little odd. It's a dreadful thing to say about a person, but——(Stops as he sees AISLA.)

(Enter AISLA.)

AISLA: Did you want me, Lady Lebanon?

LORD LEBANON: (Irritably) All this 'Lady Lebanon' stuff is rather stupid isn't it? Why not something more friendly? Why not anything reasonable and — (Catching his mother's eye.) I'm sorry.

LADY LEBANON: You can go, Willie.

49

LORD LEBANON: (Crossing to AISLA) Have you been talking to that fellow? Who does he think committed this murder? Fancy, poor old Amersham!

LADY LEBANON: Willie you can go!

LORD LEBANON: It seems to be the only thing I can do in this house. (Exits)

LADY LEBANON: What is the matter with you, Aisla?

AISLA: Nothing. (She is obviously nervous and blurts out her question.) What did you think was the matter with me? I opened the drawer of your desk this morning, and I found a little red scarf there with a metal tag on it. I don't think that ought to be there.

LADY LEBANON: Why did you open the drawer of my desk?

AISLA: I wanted the cheque-book. Why do you keep that scarf there?

LADY LEBANON: My dear child! You're dreaming. Which drawer? (AISLA points.) This one? (Opening drawer.) There's nothing there. Aisla, you mustn't let these things get on your nerves.

AISLA: (Hysterically) These things! How can you speak so lightly about it. A man killed! I hated him! I loathed him! He was always so beastly with me!

LADY LEBANON: What do you mean—was so beastly with you? Made love to you? Amersham!

AISLA: I can't go on staying here. I can't do it!

LADY LEBANON: Can't you? You've been staying here quite a long time. I sent your mother her quarterly cheque on Monday and had such a charming letter from her this morning. The two girls at school and so happy. She said how wonderful it was to feel safe and secure—after the hard times she'd been through.

50

AISLA: Don't! Please don't! It's wicked of you!
                    You know I wouldn't be here a day if it
                    wasn't for her and the girls! She doesn't
                    know what I'm doing— she'd rather starve!

LADY LEBANON: Don't be stupid, and for God's sake don't be
                    hysterical! I'm doing you a very great
                    service. When you are Lady Lebanon you'll
                    find me very broadminded about your
                    married life. You understand that? Very
                    broadminded. About that young policeman—
                    I hope you weren't in this state of nerves
                    when you were talking to him?

AISLA: (Wearily) No, of course I wasn't. He's
                    very nice.

LADY LEBANON: I'm sure he is. He talks nicely. He must
                    have gone to a good school.

AISLA: Yes— Brandell's.

LADY LEBANON: Quite an interesting public school, not of
                    the first class perhaps, but I've known
                    quite a number of very nice creatures who
                    went there. In the police force— how absurd!
                    What is his name?

AISLA: John Ferraby.

LADY LEBANON: Ferraby? One of the Somerset Ferrabys?
                    Lord Lesserfield's family? The man who
                    put the leopards in his quarterings quite
                    without authority?

AISLA: I believe he does come from Somerset.

LADY LEBANON: There's no reason why you shouldn't know
                    him, but of course you mustn't speak to
                    him about— well— about Amersham. Made
                    love to you, did he!

AISLA: He's dead now. Oh God, how awful!

LADY LEBANON: If this young man asks you questions—

AISLA: (Turning quickly.) Oh, he hasn't asked
                    me anything. We were talking about people
                    we knew. But Mr Tanner will ask me

51

AISLA: (Contd)   questions. What am I tell him?

LADY LEBANON: My dear, you will tell him just what it is necessary he should know.

(FERRABY enters.)

FERRABY: Oh, I beg your pardon. (Is about to withdraw.)

LADY LEBANON: Oh, don't go, Mr Ferraby. My niece was telling me you are related to the Lesserfields.

FERRABY: (A little embarrassed.) Well—yes, he's a sort of relation of mine, very very distant. One doesn't worry about that sort of thing when one has to earn a living.

LADY LEBANON: You should. It's the finest thing in the world to be a member — even a cadet member —of a great family. To know that your stock has continued in authority through the ages and will go on through thousands of years. Tell me, does Lord Lesserfield still quarter the leopards?

FERRABY: In his coat of arms? Yes, I believe he does.

LADY LEBANON: That is very wrong of him. Most improper! I don't think well of him for that. (Exits)

FERRABY: Good Lord! She belongs to the Middle Ages!

AISLA: She belongs to this age.

FERRABY: Or and azure—I thought that stuff was dead. Miss Crane, do you mind if I ask you a question?

AISLA: No.

FERRABY: What makes you so nervous?

AISLA: (Smiling) I told Lady Lebanon that you didn't ask me any questions.

FERRABY: And I let you down? Well, it was quite a friendly question. Why are you so jumpy?

AISLA:	Am I?
FERRABY:	You are. All the time you seem to be looking round as though you expected something horrible to appear over your shoulder.
AISLA:	(Shuddering—but forcing a laugh.) Yes, I'm afraid of the police. (Frowning) No, it's what happened last night I'm afraid of——
FERRABY:	I understand that, but you've been like this for a long time, haven't you?
AISLA:	(Turning quickly.) Who told you?
FERRABY:	Haven't you? (AISLA does not answer. Speaking more seriously.) Miss Crane, I wonder if I could help you at all? I wish I could.
AISLA:	Do you really? I suppose you want me to confide in you—officially?
FERRABY:	I ought to say yes—my job is to worm out every little secret you've got, but I'd hate myself if I did it.
AISLA:	(Smiling) Well, I have no secrets. Do you know, you're not my idea of a policeman.
FERRABY:	(Laughing) That may be very rude or very complimentary. I think I would rather it were rude.
AISLA:	And Sergeant Totty isn't my idea of a sergeant.
FERRABY:	Sergeant Totty. He's a very brave man. He got his promotion for tackling two armed burglars single-handed.
AISLA:	Yes, I can imagine that. Mr Ferraby, what do you mean when you say that you'd like to help me? What could you do for me?
FERRABY:	Well——(Pause) I could probably take away the cause of your fear. You're not

FERRABY: (Contd)	really frightened of the police, are you?
AISLA:	Of you?
FERRABY:	Well, I wasn't thinking as an individual, but as part of the machine. You can't very well be afraid of me.
AISLA:	Why not?
FERRABY:	I don't know. I suppose you could be. But you're much too sensible. Hang it all! You're not, are you?
AISLA:	No. Nor of the police. (Pause) Nor of anything.
FERRABY:	What is it?
AISLA:	There's someone coming.
	(FERRABY looks at her.)
FERRABY:	No. Are all you people afraid of being spied on? When Lord Lebanon came to Scotland Yard he had the same fear.
	(AISLA does not answer. Ferraby moves to desk.)
	There's something in this house that's got you all down. What is it?
AISLA:	(Running to desk, pushing him away—breathlessly.) Come away from that desk, please! There's nothing there. (Suddenly remembering that the scarf is gone.) There is nothing there!
	(FERRABY Looks at her, surprised.)
FERRABY:	Was there something there?
AISLA:	No! What could be there? (Turning away and speaking with her back to him.) I don't wonder you think I'm a nervous wreck. (Swinging round, facing him.) Tell me, is Mr Tanner very clever?

54

FERRABY: The best detective at Scotland Yard, I think. He has an uncanny instinct for the truth.

AISLA: I wonder ... Do you think he suspects ... (Pause) anybody?

FERRABY: Everybody, I should imagine.

AISLA: Listen! (Taking his arm.) I want to ask you something ... Suppose one knew who committed this horrible murder ... and didn't tell the police ... I mean kept it to oneself ... Is that an offence ... I mean is it ... would it be a crime? ...

FERRABY: Yes. The person who knew might be charged with being an accessory.

AISLA: Oh, my God! (Turning away quickly.)

FERRABY: Any man or woman who knows anything ought to tell. Has Tanner questioned you? (Shaking her head.) It might be easier to tell me.

AISLA: I don't know. Why should I know? You think because I'm jumpy ——

(FERRABY sniffs.)

—— these things don't get on your nerves?

FERRABY: Oh, cases like this? Well, no. It would be rather ghastly if they did, wouldn't it?

AISLA: They really don't matter to you? Isn't that strange!

FERRABY: This case matters.

AISLA: Why?

FERRABY: Well, it does—a lot.

AISLA: I suppose you've got a very matter-of-fact name for this dreadful thing: Case No. 6, or something like that?

FERRABY: No. To me it is the case of the Frightened Lady.

AISLA:	You mean me?
FERRABY:	Yes.
AISLA:	Naturally I'm frightened — my nerves aren't like yours.
	(FERRABY sniffs again.)
	What is it?
FERRABY:	A smell of something burning— a piece of cloth. (Looking down.) Has anybody dropped a cigarette on the carpet?
AISLA:	I don't know. Have they?
	(Both look down.)
FERRABY:	(Crossing to the grate and opening the stove.) Somebody's been burning stuff here — a piece of cloth. You can still see the fibre. You can smell it now, can't you?
AISLA:	No—yes— I don't know.
	(Enter TOTTY.)
TOTTY:	Hullo! What are you burning?
FERRABY:	What's that?
	(AISLA backs away.)
TOTTY:	(Crossing to the fireplace.) It looks like a bit of linen.
	(FERRABY is going to poke it with a poker.)
	Don't touch it. Do you see that little bit of metal where the corner was? It's melting, but you can see it.
FERRABY:	Yes, I see it.
TOTTY:	Phew! Where's Tanner?
FERRABY:	Upstairs somewhere.

56

TOTTY: (Turning to AISLA, who is watching, horror-stricken.) Who put that on the fire? Do you know, miss?

AISLA: (Jerkily) No. Put what on the fire?

FERRABY: It couldn't have been there long. The flame must have only just reached it when I smelt it burning.

TOTTY: Ever seen a red cloth about this house with a little metal tag in the corner?

AISLA: (Loudly) No!

TOTTY: Did you ever see anything in this house that you don't want to see again?

(AISLA looks at him and exits.)

FERRABY: (Savagely) You, I should think!

TOTTY: She looked at you, boy.

(Exit FERRABY.)

(Enter KELVER.)

KELVER: Is there something burning here?

TOTTY: Have you put anything in this stove?

KELVER: No, sir. I never replenish the fires.

TOTTY: I know, but do you.put anything on 'em?

KELVER: No, sir. Is there anything I can get for you, sir?

TOTTY: No, no. Nice old house this. Rather reminds me of Lord What's-his-name's place. I was down there for the shooting.

KELVER: Yes, sir. Lord—er——?

TOTTY: How old is this castle?

KELVER: It is very old, sir—quite historic. Queen Elizabeth lived here for a year.

TOTTY:	Go on! (Looking round with an added interest.) Did she die here?
KELVER:	No, sir, she died in London — on the 24th March, 1603.
TOTTY:	March 24, 1603. Why, that's somewhere about Grand National Day. (Pause) 1603. (Puts out his hand, shakes hands with KELVER.) I'm very much obliged to you, you've taken a great weight off my mind; in fact that's the first time I ever knew it really happened. Now, you've been so good I'm going to ask you a few more questions. Have you been here long?
KELVER:	Eighteen months, sir. I'm leaving next month.
TOTTY:	To better yourself?
KELVER:	It would hardly be respectful to her ladyship to say I was, but I do not like this part of the country; to be perfectly frank with you, sir, it hardly adds to my prestige to be associated with these crimes.
TOTTY:	Naturally. Nice lot of servants here?
KELVER:	Oh, yes, sir.
TOTTY:	Two fine strapping footmen.
KELVER:	As you say, sir, they are very strapping.
TOTTY:	Good servants, I suppose?
KELVER:	Er—well—yes. I have very little to do with them.
TOTTY:	Quate. How long have they been here?
KELVER:	They came before my time, sir.
TOTTY:	Good fellows in the servants' hall?
KELVER:	They never come to the servants' hall, sir. They go on duty when we are locked up.
TOTTY:	Oh, I see—when you're locked up. Sounds as if you got into a bit of trouble, ha ha!

58

KELVER: Oh, no , sir. The servants' quarters are in the east wing. From eight o'clock we are not in this part of the house at all.

TOTTY: Oh, I see. That's funny. You mean, you couldn't get in here if you wanted?

KELVER: Exactly, sir. It is a very — (Looking round.) —unusual arrangement to have the whole of the house cleared of servants except Gilder and Brooks. The only person who ever came here after eight o'clock was her ladyship's late maid.

TOTTY: You get many people here at nights?

KELVER: I am not able to tell you that, sir.

TOTTY: A lot of visitors, eh? I've got an idea that Dr Amersham used to call here a lot.

KELVER: I believe he did, sir. But I never saw him here at night.

TOTTY: I suppose you've heard all sorts of funny noises, haven't you?

KELVER: No, I haven't, sir.

TOTTY: Ever come down in the morning and seen signs of a barny?

KELVER: I beg your pardon?

TOTTY: Any signs of a lot of people being here, having a thick night, illicit recreation?

KELVER: Well, sir... (Hesitates) It is hardly becoming for me to discuss my employer's affairs, but there was one morning—

TOTTY: Oh?

KELVER: Well, I'll tell you the truth, sir, it looked as though there had been a free fight. Some mirrors were broken and a chair smashed and wine glasses thrown about the floor. (Looking round.) and Gilder—that is the footman—had a black eye, and I am told, though I have only got the word of poor

KELVER: (Contd)	Mr Studd to go on——
TOTTY:	That's the chauffeur who was killed?
KELVER:	Yes, poor fellow! I am told that Dr Amersham was rather the worse for wear the next day. There is certainly something happening in this house, sir, which I cannot fathom. His lordship is treated as though he had no existence; his wishes are ignored. In my opinion he is nothing better in this house than a prisoner.
TOTTY:	Oh!
KELVER:	They never let him out of their sight. (Looking round again.) I can tell you this: that I have had instructions——instructions I very much resent, though they have been given to me by her ladyship——that I have to listen to any telephone call he makes. If he has a servant he trusts, that servant is discharged. He has engaged three valets to my knowledge, and each man has been discharged on some excuse or other. The only man with whom he was friendly was Studd, who I believe, would have done anything for him—Studd was murdered. I have never expressed my suspicions before and I trust, Inspector Totty—or should I say 'sergeant'?
TOTTY:	Inspector.
KELVER:	I trust this will go no further. There's something in this house. Some dreadful force that is beginning to get on my nerves. I would gladly sacrifice a month's salary to be able to leave to-night.
	(AISLA enters hurriedly.)
TOTTY:	Anything wrong, miss?
AISLA:	No. (Looking behind her.) No!
TOTTY:	Did somebody frighten you?

AISLA:	No—nobody. I just remembered a book I wanted. (Looking round again.)
TOTTY:	Do you know you look very white?
AISLA:	Do I? (Starting round as the door opens.)

(Enter GILDER.)

GILDER:	Do you want me, miss?
AISLA:	No, I don't want you.
GILDER:	I thought I heard you call out.
AISLA:	I didn't speak.

(Enter TANNER and BROOKS.)

(To GILDER.) I don't want you to stay here. Can't you understand?

TANNER:	(Under his breath to TOTTY.) What's the matter?
TOTTY:	(Crossing to TANNER.) She came flyin' in here as if somebody was after her, and then this bird came in.
TANNER:	(Crossing to AISLA.) There's something rather wrong with you, young lady. You ought to see a doctor.
AISLA:	I don't want to see a doctor—I want—
TANNER:	What do you want?
AISLA:	I'm all right now. I was rather upset, but that's understandable, isn't it?

(Enter LADY LEBANON.)

LADY LEBANON:	Aren't you well, Aisla?
AISLA:	Oh, yes, I'm quite well, thank you.
TANNER:	(Indicating GILDER.) Did that man frighten you?

(Exit KELVER, exit GILDER upstairs.)

AISLA:	(Looking at GILDER as he goes.) No

AISLA: (Contd)	nothing frightened me, really.
LADY LEBANON:	Wouldn't you like to go to your room and lie down, Aisla?
AISLA:	No, I don't want to do that. It's nothing really.
LADY LEBANON:	(To TANNER.) Well, have you seen the house, Mr Tanner?
TANNER:	Every room except one.
BROOKS:	The lumber-room m'lady.

(LORD LEBANON enters.)

TANNER:	On the first floor, one of the best positions in the house — that's a strange place for a lumber-room.
LADY LEBANON:	We call it the lumber-room. Really, it's a store where I keep one or two valuables.
TANNER:	Your man has the key of it?
LADY LEBANON:	No. I never open that room. Mr Tanner, I'll tell you the truth. It was the room where my husband died. It hasn't been opened since that day.
LORD LEBANON:	Oh, I say, Mother! Why, I'm sure I've seen it open!
LADY LEBANON:	(Speaking very deliberately.) You are quite mistaken, Willie. That room has never been opened and you've never seen it open.
TANNER:	Well, I'd like to see it open.
LADY LEBANON:	I'm afraid you can't.
TANNER:	I'm sorry, but I must insist.
LADY LEBANON:	Be reasonable, Mr Tanner. What is there in that room that could interest you? There's nothing at all but a few pictures. I should have imagined that the scope of your inquiry lay outside of this house.

62

TANNER: The scope of my inquiry lies just where I wish it to lie, Lady Lebanon.

LORD LEBANON: Honestly, Mother, I do think he's right.

LADY LEBANON: Will you be quiet, please!

(LORD LEBANON rises, looks at LADY LEBANON and BROOKS and exits.)

TANNER: You realize, of course, that I can get a search warrant?

LADY LEBANON: It would be outrageous if you did. No magistrate in this county would grant it. (Sitting at the desk.)

(Exit BROOKS.)

TOTTY: Here!

TANNER: (Warningly) Now, my boy.

TOTTY: Here. (TANNER stops him.) If you don't mind, sir, please. I'd like to ask this lady a question. (TANNER tries to stop him again.) Who burned a scarf in that stove this afternoon?

TANNER: (Quickly) A scarf?

TOTTY: A scarf with a little metal tag in the corner.

LADY LEBANON: I haven't the slightest idea what you're talking about.

(Enter FERRABY.)

TOTTY: Why, you can smell it now. You saw it, Ferraby? The ashes are still there.

(TANNER and FERRABY cross to stove and look.)

(Enter GILDER.)

(LADY LEBANON catches AISLA's eye.)

TANNER:	Yes. I can see the metal tag melting on the coal. (Looking at LADY LEBANON.) Well?...
LADY LEBANON:	If something has been burnt I haven't the least idea who burnt it, or what it was. Do you know, Gilder?
GILDER:	I'm afraid I'm responsible, my lady. I found some odd bits and ends of silk lying on the carpet and I put them in the stove.
LADY LEBANON:	Oh, of course. I was cutting out a doll's dress for the village bazaar. You remember, Aisla?
	(AISLA does not answer. She stiffens.)
	It was very foolish of you to put those pieces into the fire, Gilder.
TANNER:	I see. Ferraby, take Miss Crane out, will you?
	(There is a dead silence while FERRABY and AISLA exit.)
TOTTY:	There's another thing I'd like to know.
TANNER:	Perhaps I'll find it out for you. All right, my friend. (Nods to GILDER, who bows and exits.)(To TOTTY under his breath.) Follow that man and keep your eye on him.
TOTTY:	You know I could be a lot of help to you.
TANNER:	Don't let that man out of your sight.
TOTTY:	Don't throw away your opportunities, boy. (He bows to LADY LEBANON and exits.)
LADY LEBANON:	Do I understand you have something to ask me?
TANNER:	Yes.
LADY LEBANON:	Well, what is it about?
TANNER:	Curiously enough, it's about the murder of Dr Amersham. That's why I'm here.

64

TANNER: (Contd) No other reason except to investigate the murder by strangulation of Dr Leicester Amersham.

LADY LEBANON: I think I've told you everything I know.

TANNER: I've never had that illusion. Lady Lebanon, when did you last see Dr Amersham alive?

LADY LEBANON: I didn't see him this morning.

TANNER: That I realize. He wasn't alive this morning. The medical evidence is that he was killed last night, probably about midnight. When did you see him last alive?

LADY LEBANON: Yesterday morning, or it may have been the day before. I'm not quite sure.

TANNER: He was here at eleven last night—probably until within a few minutes of his death. He was here in this room talking to you.

LADY LEBANON: You've been questioning my servants?

TANNER: Naturally.

LADY LEBANON: I think it would have been a little more polite if you'd come to me first.

TANNER: Well, I have come to you and you've told me it was yesterday morning you saw him, or it may have been the day before. Here is a man murdered — rather an impressive face.

LADY LEBANON: I don't follow you.

TANNER: If you had a friend who met with a fatal accident soon after you saw him, wouldn't you say immediately, 'Why, I was only speaking to him an hour before!'

LADY LEBANON: Dr Amersham was not a friend. He was rather a self-willed man who saw nobody's point of view but his own.

TANNER: So the fact that he was murdered within a few hundred yards of this room really doesn't matter.

65

LADY LEBANON: That is a little insolent, Mr Tanner.

TANNER: Yes, I suppose it is. Doesn't it strike you, Lady Lebanon, that your own attitude is peculiar — I won't say arrogant? I'm a detective officer, investigating the murder of Dr Amersham. You tell me you cannot remember when you saw him last, although he was with you up to a few moments of his death. You suggest that you cannot fix the time, because he was not a friend of yours but just a self-willed man. That seems a little inadequate, doesn't it? If he wasn't a friend, what was he doing here at eleven?

LADY LEBANON: He came to see me.

TANNER: As a doctor?

LADY LEBANON: Yes.

TANNER: At your request?

LADY LEBANON: No. He dropped in.

TANNER: At eleven o'clock at night?

LADY LEBANON: I had a touch of neuritis in my arm.

TANNER: But you didn't send for him?

LADY LEBANON: No.

TANNER: He just guessed you had neuritis and drove down from London in his car to treat you? Did he write a prescription?

LADY LEBANON: That is a matter which concerns me—and I will not discuss it.

TANNER: He left you at twelve and drove down—the Long Avenue, that's what you call it, isn't it? Half-way down somebody who must have been in the car strangled him as he sat at the wheel.

LADY LEBANON: I know nothing whatever about that.

TANNER: The car from which he was evidently dragged was found abandoned at the other side of the village.

66

LADY LEBANON: Really, I'm not interested.

TANNER: Lady Lebanon! You've known this gentleman for years; he was a constant visitor —
your own doctor, and friend, and you're not
interested in his brutal murder?

LADY LEBANON: I'm terribly sorry, of course. It was an
awful thing to have happened.

TANNER: I'm glad you think that. (Deliberately)
What did Dr Amersham know?

LADY LEBANON: I don't understand you.

TANNER: Your last words to the doctor as he left the
door were these; you stood there, you spoke
in an angry voice and you said: 'Nobody
would believe you if you told them. Tell
them if you dare! And don't forget that you
are as deeply in it as anybody. You've
always wanted to handle Willie's money.'
(Silence) They may not be the exact words,
but they are the sense of the words. What
was he 'deeply in'? (Silence) What did you
dare him to tell?

LADY LEBANON: Celia Clark told you of course — my maid.
She's an utterly dishonest and untrust-
worthy girl and I've discharged her. If you
listen to discharged servants, Mr Tanner—

TANNER: I listen to anybody — that's my job. How
long was your husband, the late Lord
Lebanon, ill before he died?

LADY LEBANON: Fifteen years.

TANNER: Who attended him?

LADY LEBANON: (Reluctantly) Dr Amersham.

TANNER: (Consulting notebook.) Although he was ill
so long he died rather suddenly, didn't he?
I've got the particulars of the certificate
here. It's signed by Leicester Amersham,
M.B.,L.R.C.P.,M.R.C.S. (Puts away notebook and produces red envelope with
marriage certificate.) During his

67

TANNER: (Contd)   illness you administered his affairs? You
and Dr Amersham?

      (LADY LEBANON nods.)

      (Pause) Why did you marry again?

LADY LEBANON: That isn't true!

TANNER: Why did you marry Leicester Charles
Amersham at the Peterfield Parish Church
three months after your husband's death?

      (LADY LEBANON does not answer.)

      And why did you keep the marriage secret?

LADY LEBANON: Who told you?

TANNER: Somerset House told me. (Replacing
paper in envelope and putting both in his
pocket.)

LADY LEBANON: It was forced on me. Dr Amersham
was an adventurer of the lowest kind. He
blackmailed me into marriage.

TANNER: How?

LADY LEBANON: He blackmailed me — that's enough.

TANNER: What hold did he have on you?

      (There is no answer.)

      You know you can't blackmail people
unless you know something to their
detriment.

LADY LEBANON: I shall not tell you.

TANNER: Had you broken the law?

LADY LEBANON: I know that he had — he was a thief and a
forger.

TANNER: He was here last night at twelve. He
threatened you and was killed a few
minutes later, and you're not very
interested?

LADY LEBANON: Why should I be? I'm glad he's — (Stopping suddenly.)

68

TANNER: You're glad he's dead? And then you suddenly remembered something, and you weren't so glad?

LADY LEBANON: That's absurd!

TANNER: Now, as to your first husband, Mrs Amersham—

LADY LEBANON: (Stiffening) I shall be glad if you will call me Lady Lebanon.

TANNER: Who saw the late Lord Lebanon after his death?

LADY LEBANON: Dr Amersham.

TANNER: Did you?

LADY LEBANON: No.

TANNER: Did anybody else?

LADY LEBANON: Gilder and Brooks.

TANNER: Nobody else?

LADY LEBANON: No—they did everything. No outsider was called in.

TANNER: I see. (Looking at the certificate.) And the doctor signed the certificate. Hm. This morning my interest in this was academic—except that I was interested in Dr Amersham. Now I'm very interested in you and in this house—and in the room which, you say, is never opened. Have you got the key? (Puts out his hand.)

(LADY LEBANON does not answer.)

(With sudden geniality.) Oh, well, I'm probably worrying you unnecessarily, I should have liked to have seen the room. I'm an inquisitive man I've got an idea—I may be wrong—that Dr Amersham's hold over you had something to do with that room. Now, aren't I right?

LADY LEBANON: No! It had something to do... with my past.

69

TANNER: (Shaking his head.) It took an effort to say that, and it isn't true. You're one of those people one reads about—blood proud. By the way, you must be a Lebanon yourself?

LADY LEBANON: (With a smile.) How clever of you to realize that. Yes, I married my cousin. I go back in direct line to the fourth baron.

TANNER: Amazing!

LADY LEBANON: The family has come from most ancient times, Mr Tanner; before there was a history of England there was a history of the Lebanons, and it will go on! It must go on! It would be wicked if the line were broken!

TANNER: Amazing!

LADY LEBANON: You said that before, Mr Tanner. (Rising, standing at the desk and ringing the bell.)

TANNER: (Looking at his watch.) I don't think I can do very much more to-night. I have a few inquiries to make in the village.

LADY LEBANON: (Obviously relieved.) Perhaps if you come tomorrow, we'll show you our mysterious room.

(GILDER enters and stands watching.)

(AISLA enters.)

TANNER: I'll collect my men. It's getting dusk. I'd rather not walk across the Priory Field in the dark.

AISLA: (Tremulously) Are you going, Mr Tanner?

LADY LEBANON: Mr Tanner is staying at the White Hart.

(Enter KELVER.)

(Turning to him.) Oh, Kelver! Will you put this into the safe? (Handing him the portfolio, moving to stairs and going up.)

AISLA: (Close to TANNER—intensely.) Don't go to-night! For God's sake, don't go!

LADY LEBANON: Have you got a car, Mr Tanner?

TANNER: I've decided not to go just yet. I hope you don't mind?

QUICK CURTAIN

ACT II

Scene 2

The SCENE is the same.   Night.   The lamps are lit.

                    (TANNER is speaking on the telephone.)

TANNER:
           I want to get the warrant down here tomorrow by nine o'clock if it's possible. Yes, I think I've got to the bottom of it... It is a bit delicate, but I think I can handle it, sir... Yes, sir... I'd like the order I asked for, but I think it would be advisable to send down three of the best men you can get, if you don't mind my suggesting that, sir... The Public Prosecutor's department will know all about it...No, no, no! What Lord Lebanon said, just as he was going out of my room at Scotland Yard was: 'I hope you'll come to the Priory and I hope I'll be alive to see you'. ... No, he's not said anything. I haven't had much of a chance to talk to him. Thank you, sir. (Smiling) A kind word from you is always acceptable! Oh, I know... Of course... Thank you very much... Good night sir. (Hanging up receiver.)

           (LORD LEBANON is heard speaking off stage: 'No, no, Mr Totty, I don't agree at all...')

           (LORD LEBANON and SERGEANT TOTTY enter.)

LORD LEBANON:
           I have always thought that the whole House of Lords system was perfectly ridiculous. I mean, it isn't democratic.

TOTTY:
           Yes, I see your point.

TANNER:	Have you ever taken your seat in the Lords, Lord Lebanon?
LORD LEBANON:	No, I ... haven't. The fact is, my mother —er—she's not terribly keen on my going into politics at all for a year or two. I'm awfully glad you're staying to-night. (Looking round and lowering his voice.) I'm afraid my mother isn't glad. She was fearfully angry with me and said I was responsible, which, of course, I wasn't.
TANNER:	Where's Miss Crane?
LORD LEBANON:	She's gone to bed, I think. She's not terribly sociable. I'm going to have a very dull time when I'm married. She goes to bed so early. She's awfully kind and all that, but honestly, we have nothing in common. I'll tell you who are sick about your staying—these two......
	(TANNER motions him to be quiet.)
	(GILDER enters.)
	I don't want you, Gilder.
GILDER:	I was going to look at the fire, my lord. (Crossing to the fire.)
TANNER:	(Addressing GILDER, who does not take any notice of him.) What time do you go to bed?
LORD LEBANON:	Gilder! Mr Tanner is speaking to you.
GILDER:	I beg your pardon. (Turning round.) I thought you were addressing his lordship. I've no regular hours, sir.
TANNER:	Do you sleep in this part of the house?
GILDER:	When I sleep, I sleep in this part of the house.
	(Enter BROOKS. LORD LEBANON looks at him, then at TANNER significantly.)

73

TANNER: It sounds as if you didn't sleep very well.

GILDER: On the contrary, sir. When I sleep, I sleep extremely well.

TANNER: (To BROOKS.) Do you want anything?

BROOKS: I just wanted to see Gilder wasn't getting into trouble.

TANNER: I'm not quite sure whether you're being flippant because I'm an unimportant visitor, or whether that is your natural manner.

GILDER: Mr Brooks comes from the States, the home of the free. From the wide, open spaces where men are men.

BROOKS: You've said it.

TANNER: (Rising and moving to GILDER.) When people get fresh with me I sometimes put them in a space which is neither wide nor open, and certainly isn't free.

GILDER: Have I said anything that's an offence within the meaning of the act?

TANNER: It's not an offence, but suppose I took rather a dislike to you two men, and I decided that you knew a great deal more than you're prepared to admit. Suppose I was to hold you as accessories and take you down to the station to-night? You aren't smiling? That would be a little embarrassing, wouldn't it?

GILDER: I beg your pardon. I'm afraid I allowed my sense of humour to get the better of me. I'd no intention of being offensive.

TANNER: (Turning to BROOKS.) How do you feel about it?

BROOKS: Why, I guess I feel the same as Gilder. You don't want me, my lord?

LORD LEBANON: No. I didn't send for you, did I?

74

LORD LEBANON: (Contd)   (Exit BROOKS.)

(To GILDER.) Bring us some drinks.

GILDER: Certainly. What would you like — a whisky and soda? Shall I bring one for you, Mr Tanner?

TANNER: (With a nod.) Yes.

(GILDER is about to exit.)

TOTTY: I'm here.

(Exit GILDER.)

TANNER: (To LORD LEBANON.) Do you remember telling me this morning that you hoped to be alive to see me if I came to Mark's Priory? What did you mean by that? Have you had any sort of threat or has anybody attempted to hurt you?

LORD LEBANON: No, not directly, but——(Suddenly stopping.)

TOTTY: There was a jamboree here one night— somebody smashed the furniture and broke up the glass.

LORD LEBANON: Yes—I know about that.

TANNER: When was this?

TOTTY: Some time ago. The place looked as if there'd been a pretty wild party, didn't it? (To TANNER.) You see, it took me to find that out!

LORD LEBANON: I wish there were a few wild parties! Good Lord! This place is like a mausoleum, and after the wonderful time I had in India! You know, I've hardly spoken to a girl since I've been back, except Aisla?

TANNER: Have you a picture of your father?

LORD LEBANON:	It's funny that you should ask that—no. There isn't one in the house. I came across a snapshot taken in the grounds—he was in his invalid chair. It must have been taken a couple of years before he died. Mother snatched it out of my hand and burned it.
TANNER:	That was a funny thing to do, wasn't it?
LORD LEBANON:	I tell you she's a dear, but she's odd. Of course, it was an awful-looking picture of him, but can you understand it?
TANNER:	Yes. If it was an awful-looking picture I think I can understand it.
TOTTY:	I'd like to ask you a question. Have they ever kept you out of the way? I mean, have you ever had a feeling of being kept out of the way while something was on?
LORD LEBANON:	Oh, good Lord, yes! Yes. And I'll tell you how they keep me out of the way. You asked me about the party. I was in here after dinner one night, and Gilder brought me a whisky and soda. I remember drinking it and the next thing I remember was waking up in my room, absolutely in the dark. The door was locked. I tried to get out. I had a perfectly splitting headache. When they came up to me, they said that I'd fainted. I've never fainted in my life. That was the night of the party! They tried to tidy up before I got down, but they couldn't hide it all. There used to be an old china clock there (Pointing)—that was smashed, and a case full of miniatures, and mother had to get another carpet.
TOTTY:	(To TANNER.) There you are!
TANNER:	Did they explain what had happened?
LORD LEBANON:	Not a word.
	(LADY LEBANON enters.)

76

LORD LEBANON:
(Contd)
They said that one of the servants had upset something.

LADY LEBANON: Why aren't you in bed, Willie? Where's Gilder?

(The men have risen.)

LORD LEBANON: I've sent him for a drink, Mother.

TANNER: I am afraid we're being a nuisance to you, Lady Lebanon.

LADY LEBANON: I'm afraid you are. You'd have been so much more comfortable at the White Hart. (Looking round.) Where's Mr Ferraby? I hope he's been a sensible man and gone to the inn.

TANNER: Ferraby's making a few inquiries in the village. He'll be back very soon.

(Enter GILDER with a tray. The whisky is already poured out in glasses.)

LORD LEBANON: (Angrily) How often have I told you to bring in the decanter and the siphon?

LADY LEBANON: Willie!

LORD LEBANON: Damn it all, Mother! It isn't civilized! (Taking the drink which GILDER hands him.)

LADY LEBANON: Have you discovered anything new, Mr Tanner?

TANNER: Nothing at all.

LADY LEBANON: Willie, I think you should go to bed.

LORD LEBANON: All right, Mother. In a few minutes.

LADY LEBANON: Gilder. (She exits followed by GILDER.)

LORD LEBANON: (Sipping his drink.) I say, just taste this, will you?

(TANNER tastes the whisky, and makes a wry face.)

77

TANNER: What is it?

LORD LEBANON: I've tasted stuff like that before. Bitter?

TANNER: Yes.

LORD LEBANON: Does yours taste bitter?

TANNER: No.

                 (LORD LEBANON pours the contents of
                 his glass into the bowl of flowers on the
                 table in front of the sofa.)

LORD LEBANON: There's something on to-night—they want
                 me out of the way. I wonder what they're
                 going to do to you?

TOTTY: They'll do nothing to us.

LORD LEBANON: Don't be too sure. Amersham was
                 confident that nothing could happen to him.

                 (Re-enter LADY LEBANON followed by
                 GILDER.)

LADY LEBANON: Willie, have you finished your drink? Go
                 to bed, darling.

LORD LEBANON: (Rising) Oh, all right.

TANNER: Which is your room, Lord Lebanon? I
                 was shown it this morning, but I've
                 forgotten where it is.

LORD LEBANON: I'll show it to you. (To LADY LEBANON.)
                 May I?

LADY LEBANON: Of course.

                 (LORD LEBANON, TANNER and TOTTY
                 exit.)

                 Do you think we can get rid of these men?

GILDER: I'm afraid not. Brooks is getting cold
                 feet. He says he's going to quit. These
                 detectives are scaring him.

LADY LEBANON: Do they scare you?

GILDER:	(With a smile and shake of his head.) No, nothing scares me. I'm in now and I'll go through with it.
LADY LEBANON:	Tell Brooks that there will be a thousand pounds for him if we get this thing over without any discovery.
GILDER:	Do you think we will?
LADY LEBANON:	Of course.
	(Re-enter TANNER.)
	(To TANNER.) You know your rooms? I suppose you'll wait up for Mr Ferraby? Good night. I'll leave you to lock up, Gilder.
GILDER:	Yes, my lady.
LADY LEBANON:	If you want to get into the grounds in the night, there's a small door here into the rose garden. I'll show it to you.
TANNER:	Thank you.
	(Exit LADY LEBANON and TANNER.)
	(GILDER comes down to small table, looks at empty glass, examines it, frowns; sees the bowl on the table, picks it up and smells it. Pause.)
	(Enter BROOKS down the stairs.)
GILDER:	He didn't drink that stuff.
BROOKS:	Sure he didn't drink it. You made it too strong. I told you he'd taste it.
GILDER:	He's getting wise to it. Has he been talking?
BROOKS:	Yuh! Somebody told him about the rough house and Tanner questioned the boy. He knew he'd been doped. That's serious. Did you speak to her?
GILDER:	Yea. There's nothing to worry about.

79

BROOKS: Like Hell! There's a whole lot to worry about. I don't like these English cops. They're getting wise to what's been going on here. I'm scared, I tell you. If the truth comes out we're in it up to here. We might get a lifer for this.

GILDER: Quiet!

(TOTTY enters down the stairs.)

TOTTY: Hullo! The brothers Mick and Muck.

GILDER: Is there something I can do for you, sir?

(BROOKS is making an awkward attempt to appear tidying. He collects the glasses, puts them on a tray and is going to take them out.)

TOTTY: No, thank you. I suppose you'll be up all night?

GILDER: If you'll be up all night, sir, I'll be up all night.

(Exit BROOKS.)

TOTTY: Does it ever strike you blokes that you might get yourselves into a bit of trouble?

GILDER: Man is born to trouble as the sparks fly upward.

TOTTY: Saucy dog! (Goes to the door as if to follow and is looking after him.)

(LADY LEBANON re-enters.)

LADY LEBANON: Ah, Mr Totty!

TOTTY: Ah, my Lady!

LADY LEBANON: Mr Tanner has gone into the garden. I hope you will be comfortable.

80

TOTTY: Thank you very kindly. (LADY
                    LEBANON starts to leave.) Sleep well.

LADY LEBANON: Mr Totty, I was quite rude to you this
                    evening.

TOTTY: A mere bagatelle.

LADY LEBANON: I'm very sorry, but I was a little <u>distraite.</u>

TOTTY: It's the weather.

LADY LEBANON: (Rather taken aback.) Yes, I suppose so.
                    You're a sergeant, aren't you?

TOTTY: Temporarily.

LADY LEBANON: Mr Tanner is——?

TOTTY: Chief Superintendent. (Indifferently) Well,
                    there's practically no difference between
                    us, merely a matter of rank.

LADY LEBANON: Will you forgive me if I ask you whether
                    you receive a very large salary? I
                    suppose you do. Yours must be very
                    important work.

TOTTY: Well, it is <u>important,</u> you know, but they
                    try to crab it.

LADY LEBANON: To—— Oh, yes, to disparage it?

TOTTY: Er——yes.

LADY LEBANON: (Looking at TOTTY.) I should like to know
                    just what is happening ... and what the
                    police think about this case. I suppose
                    there are things arising every few
                    minutes...clues... or whatever you call
                    them?

TOTTY: (On a level with LADY LEBANON.) Oh
                    yes—I've had a few meself.

LADY LEBANON: Have you?

TOTTY: Well, in a way.

LADY LEBANON: I suppose when you make a new discovery
                    you tell Mr Tanner? Then what does he
                    say?

TOTTY:	Usually he says he's known all about that for a week. There's a lot of petty jealousy in the Service.
LADY LEBANON:	But I suppose he does place a lot of reliance on you?
TOTTY:	Naturally. I'm his right hand, so to speak.
LADY LEBANON:	He was very curious—rather stupidly so, I thought—about that room I didn't want him to see. Do you remember? Perhaps he's not quite as clever as you.
TOTTY:	Well, we ought to be fair to the man.
LADY LEBANON:	Suppose you went to him and said: 'I've been into this room and there's nothing there but a few old pictures.' That would satisfy him, wouldn't it? He does take a lot of notice of what you say?
TOTTY:	Yes. Sometimes an awful lot—sometimes a fat lot.
LADY LEBANON:	(Silkily) Suppose you did say there was nothing in the room. It would save me a lot of bother.
TOTTY:	Quate.
LADY LEBANON:	(Opening a drawer and counting notes as she speaks.) One feels so perfectly helpless against trained and skilful men from Scotland Yard. Very naturally they see something suspicious in the most innocent actions and it's nice to know that one has a friend at court. (Placing notes prominently on desk, then rising.) Good night, Sergeant Totty. (Going)
TOTTY:	Good night, my lady. (Seeing notes and picking them up.) One moment! You've left your money behind.
LADY LEBANON:	(Deliberately) I don't remember leaving any money behind.
TOTTY:	(Hands the notes to her.) Well, that will remind you. You never know when you

82

TOTTY: (Contd)   may want it.

LADY LEBANON: I was hoping you might want it too. (Going) It's rather a pity.

(Re-enter TANNER.)

TANNER: What's rather a pity?

TOTTY: That I don't want a couple of hundred pounds. Ha ha! She doesn't want that room opened.

TANNER: Lady Lebanon? I never imagined she did. And she offered you money?

TOTTY: She left it behind.

TANNER: What did you say?

TOTTY: Oh, I told her she mustn't do anything like that, that I was a sergeant, who'd probably get a promotion out of this case— in fact it's been practically promised to me, hasn't it?

TANNER: No!

TOTTY: Oh! I said: 'I'm surprised at you, I am really!'

TANNER: (Obviously sceptical.) And what did she say?

TOTTY: Well, what could she say? Burst into tears and went upstairs.

TANNER: It sounds like a lie, but there may be some truth in it. She doesn't want that room opened. (Nodding and smiling.) Well, we'll open it to-morrow.

TOTTY: Do you know what you'll find? (Eagerly) Stacks of booze! I got it from the first. Why American footmen?

TANNER: I'll tell you why American footmen—because they've got no friends in England—no families. She's taking no risk about their talking.

83

TOTTY: Will you remember I put you wise to
           that? Don't take all the credit, boy. I've
           seen what's wrong here from the first.

TANNER: What have you seen?

           (Enter GILDER carrying a tray, with
           a whisky decanter, siphon of soda and
           glasses, which he places on the desk.)

GILDER: I thought I'd bring this in case you
           required it. (Opening cigar-box.) Perhaps
           you'd like to smoke——

TANNER: Thank you.

           (Exit GILDER.)

TOTTY: He's the brains of the party.

TANNER: I can understand you think like that. Well,
           what's your theory?

TOTTY: They're using this place as headquarters
           for a gang; what do you think of that idea?

TANNER: Lousy. What do they want a gang for when
           they've all the picking in the world?
           Lebanon paid over three hundred thousand
           pounds in death duties.

TOTTY: It costs 'em a bit to die, don't it?

           (FERRABY enters.)

TANNER: Hullo! Well?

FERRABY: You were quite right about Amersham.
           He's got a foul reputation in the village.
           He's been paying alimony to quite a number
           of unofficial wives. I saw one of them to-
           night. That man had everything except taste.
           (Taking out notebook.) Do you want particu-
           lars.

TANNER: No, they'll do in the morning. I wonder if
           she knew?

TOTTY:	Who?
TANNER:	(To FERRABY.) Help yourself to a drink.
FERRABY:	(Shaking his head.) No, thanks. I suppose Miss Crane has gone to bed?
TOTTY:	She asked me to kiss you good night.
FERRABY:	Horrible, isn't it?
TANNER:	What? —Totty?
FERRABY:	No, this place. (Shuddering)
TOTTY:	I don't know, boy. I've seen worse. (To TANNER.) Do you remember that night we spent in the cat's-meat shop—waitin' for Harry the Fiddler? (Drinking) Gawd! cats used to follow me about for weeks after.
FERRABY:	Oh, I don't know, I prefer almost any-where to this place – the whole house seems full of ghosts!
TANNER:	(Listening) Quiet!
	(A shadow appears on the wall. Gradually AISLA comes into view. She is wearing a nightdress and a negligee. Obviously she is walking in her sleep. She comes down into the room. She goes to LADY LEBANON's desk, opens a drawer and fumbles in it.)
AISLA:	The cloth is here. It ought to be burnt! It ought to be burnt!
	(FERRABY tries to go towards her, but TANNER holds him back. AISLA walks back to where she came, talking as she moves.)
	Where is the cloth—it ought to be burnt! It ought to be burnt! You killed him with that... I saw you come into the house with it... in your hand... It must be burnt...

AISLA: (Contd)   Where is that cloth. . . it was here. . . It
                  must be burnt. . . I saw it in your hand. . .

                  (They watch her go.)

                  CURTAIN

ACT III

Scene 1

A Bedroom. The window is heavily curtained, a dressing-
table is in front of it, with a chair. A large four-post bedstead.
A central door. A trick panel between the door and the bed.
The light switch is above the table.

(AISLA is sleeping. A nightlight is
burning by the side of her bed. Three
separate knocks at the door. They are
repeated. AISLA wakes, sits up, looks
about her, gets out of bed and puts on
negligée, then goes to door.)

AISLA: Who is it?

LADY LEBANON: (Off) It's Lady Lebanon.

(AISLA opens door. Enter LADY
LEBANON. She is fully dressed as in
Act II, Scene 2.)

AISLA: (Returning to bed.) Is anything the matter?

LADY LEBANON: No. (Closing the door.) Do you always sleep
with that light on?

AISLA: Yes. Lately.

LADY LEBANON: It's very bad for you.

AISLA: I loathe this room.

LADY LEBANON: (Turning on light.) You've never said so
before. One room is as good as another.

AISLA: It's got secret doors, hasn't it? I heard
Mr Tanner talking about it.

LADY LEBANON: I thought you knew that.

AISLA: Where are they? Show me.

87

LADY LEBANON: I don't know them all. The man who planned this room lived a hundred years ago. He was rather eccentric—he never saw anybody. They used to pass his meals through a panel. There used to be a passage-way here in the very heart of the wall.

AISLA: It gives me such an ugly feeling.

LADY LEBANON: Courcy Lebanon - that was his name. He married a Hanshaw. Her mother was a blood relation of Monmouth. That branch has died out. Aisla, I want to talk to you. You must wake up!

AISLA: I'm so awfully tired.

(LADY LEBANON goes to door, re-locks it.)

Why did you do that?

LADY LEBANON: You walked in your sleep to-night.

AISLA: Did I? I wish I didn't. I never did that before——(Stopping)

LADY LEBANON: Before what?

AISLA: Before that terrible night ... when the furniture was broken and Dr Amersham— (Shudders) I thought he was killed.

LADY LEBANON: If you hadn't come down, you'd have seen nothing.

AISLA: (With her head in her hands.) What time is it?

LADY LEBANON: Half-past two.

AISLA: Haven't you been to bed?

LADY LEBANON: No. (At bedside—urgently.) Aisla, anything may happen to-morrow. I may be—(Shrugs) I hope it can be avoided, but I must be prepared. Aisla, I want you to marry Willie. Do you hear? I want you to marry Willie?

AISLA:	(Half asleep.) When?
LADY LEBANON:	To-morrow——to-day that is.
AISLA:	(Looking up, wondering.) What did you say—marry? But we couldn't marry at such short notice?
LADY LEBANON:	I've had the licence for a week.
AISLA:	(Shaking her head.) I can't.
LADY LEBANON:	Oh yes, you can.
AISLA:	He'd hate it.
LADY LEBANON:	He'll do as I tell him.
AISLA:	Why to-day?
LADY LEBANON:	Aisla, Willie is the last of the Lebanons— the last link in the chain. A weak link. There was another weak link —— Geoffrey Lebanon—he was a weaker link than Willie. He married his cousin Jane Secamore—you'll see her portrait in the Great Hall. She left him at the atlar, but she had several children.
AISLA:	What a horrible idea! How dreadful!
LADY LEBANON:	I don't agree. Jane was the greatest of the Lebanon women. You realize you're a Lebanon. Whatever happens, your children will be Lebanons; when you're married to Willie they'll bear the Lebanon name, the line will go on. If you find your married life with Willie impossible, you'll find me very understanding.
AISLA:	I can't realize what it means. I can't do it! I can't do it!
LADY LEBANON:	You not only can do it——
AISLA:	(Rising) I won't do it.
LADY LEBANON:	Aisla! You will be doing a wonderful thing —you shall found a new race. The family will find a new strength. The Lebanon women have always been greater than the men.

AISLA:	(Starts—and looks at door.) There's somebody in the corridor! (They listen.) who is it?
LADY LEBANON:	S-sh! It's Gilder, I think. He's been outside your door all the evening. These men are getting out of control. I may not hold them after to-night. That's another reason. Gilder mustn't know you're going to be married. That's the one thing he mustn't know. You understand?

(AISLA nods—half asleep.)

(LADY LEBANON goes to door, opens it. GILDER is there.)

Do you want me, Gilder?

GILDER:	Yes. (Showing her scarf.) Look at this—

(Exit LADY LEBANON and GILDER, talking.)

(AISLA goes to door, opens it, goes out, sees something on the ground, picks it up, brings it into the room, closes the door, stands with her back to it and examines the scarf. She is dazed, blinking. Again examines scarf and goes to table by bed, staggering with tiredness, puts scarf on table. Takes off negligée and gets into bed.

When she is still, GILDER puts hand through secret panel, takes handkerchief, shuts panel.

Pause.

GILDER knocks 7 times on door.

Short pause.

GILDER enters slowly, stands facing bed.)

GILDER:	The door wasn't locked after all!
BROOKS:	(Off) No.

90

GILDER: (Looking towards AISLA.) You must come with me, young lady, and don't make a noise.

(Pause—goes to bed—bends over and looks at AISLA.)

(Over his shoulder.) By God, she's asleep; would you believe it?

(BROOKS enters with a blanket over his arm.)

BROOKS: Hurry! (He is very nervous.) There are twenty damned ways into this room.

GILDER: S-sh! (At bed.) She's dead asleep.

BROOKS: If you touch her she'll wake, and if she wakes, she'll raise hell.

(AISLA stirs.)

GILDER: Quiet! (Standing back against wall.)

(AISLA turns in her bed, sits up, faces out to the audience, eyes almost shut.)

AISLA: (Feebly)   I can't do it! You know I can't do it!

GILDER: She's right out. (Pause) Give me that rug. (Takes rug, puts the rug round AISLA's shoulders, and sits above her on bed, his left arm round her, holding the rug.)

BROOKS: If you wake her she'll—

GILDER: She won't wake. Go outside and see if anybody is about. If she'd been doped she couldn't be sleeping heavier.

BROOKS: Did you give her a spot? (GILDER shakes his head.) Where are you going to take her?

GILDER: To my room.

BROOKS:	Does the old woman know?
GILDER:	To hell with the old woman! I'm going to have <u>my</u> way to-night.
BROOKS:	Where is she?
GILDER:	Look out again.

(BROOKS goes out and returns.)

BROOKS:	If there's any trouble to-night, I'll shoot! I'm not taking any more risks. (Putting his hand on his hip.) God, it's gone!
GILDER:	Your gun? You were a damn' fool to have it on you. Are you sure you had it?
BROOKS:	Yeah. I had it all right. Phew!

(They look at each other.)

GILDER:	And all the world knew you had it. I warned you about it. S-sh!

(AISLA stirs—gets up. GILDER rises. Follows her.)

AISLA:	(Walks out—asleep—talking.) Where is that cloth.
GILDER:	Give me those slippers, and stay here and straighten out the bed.

(BROOKS gives GILDER the slippers and dressing-gown, shuts the door, and tidies the bed. GILDER puts hand through panel and turns off light-switch.)

(BLACK OUT.)

BROOKS:	Gilder! Gilder! Put on the light! (Makes choking noise and falls.)

QUICK CURTAIN, as he falls

92

ACT III

Scene 2

The Prior's Hall.

>(TOTTY is seated, playing Patience at
>the desk. TANNER enters and looks
>around.)

TANNER: A man who can cheat himself at patience is a crook at heart.

TOTTY: A man who can't make things go as he wants them is a damn' fool!

TANNER: Has anything happened?

TOTTY: No. I thought I heard something moving upstairs, but I couldn't see anybody.

TANNER: So did I.

TOTTY: What did you come down for? Don't you trust me, Hubert?

TANNER: I can't sleep.

TOTTY: I wouldn't have your conscience for a lot of money.

TANNER: The seven goes there. (Points)

TOTTY: I knew that. I was waiting to see the best place to put it.

TANNER: The best place for a red seven is on a black eight.

TOTTY: (Scrambles up the cards.) March 24th, 1603.

TANNER: Is that the date of your birth or your discharge from the Army?

TOTTY: I ought to get a rank over this job, you know Tanner. Practically all that's been discovered is due to me. Who found out that Gilder had a bank account, eh?

TANNER:	I did.
TOTTY:	Well, in this case you're right, which only shows what chance I've got.
TANNER:	Where are the footmen?
TOTTY:	I haven't seen 'em for nearly an hour. Here, one of those fellows carries a gun. The one who chews gum all the while. I saw the shape of it when he took off his coat to tidy up.
TANNER:	Carries a gun, does he?
TOTTY:	He's going to be a bit of trouble when we pinch him.
TANNER:	Have you seen her ladyship?
TOTTY:	(In his refined tones.) She was down here half an hour ago. Very affable. As a matter of fact, she gave me these cards. Very posh, aren't they? I suppose you can lose money with them same as you can with the common ones?
TANNER:	(Without looking round.) Which room is Miss Crane sleeping in?
TOTTY:	Haven't you found that out? You've lost a bit of dash, haven't you? It's the old-fashioned room with the four-poster in it.
TANNER:	The Old Lord's room. Oh yes. A gloomy-looking place for a girl. I'd hate to sleep there.
TOTTY:	Would you? Well, everybody to his fancy. Where's Ferraby?
TANNER:	He's in the grounds. I let him out through the garden door, just before I went to bed.
TOTTY:	Better him than me, I'm glad he's not sitting up. I don't want to talk about Miss Crane all night.
	(Both look up.)
	That's somebody.

TANNER:	Go up and see.
TOTTY:	Don't be silly! You told me to stay down here.
TANNER:	(Contemptuously) Are you frightened?
TOTTY:	Yes. That surprises you, don't it? Still, just to oblige you.
	(Taking a torch from his pocket he exits, nervously.)
	(Off) Here, Tanner, quick!
GILDER:	(Off) Is something wrong?
TANNER:	What's happening?
GILDER:	(Off) O.K., I can get him down.
	(TOTTY and GILDER bring in BROOKS. He is half conscious, and his collar is torn open. GILDER stands in front of BROOKS, in chair, and takes red scarf from his neck, puts scarf in pocket.)
TANNER:	Where did you find him?
TOTTY:	Inside Miss Crane's room. I rushed in and trod on him! Miss Crane's gone!
TANNER:	Where is she?
GILDER:	She's somewhere in the house. Very likely she's changed her room—she was kinda nervous to-night.
TOTTY:	The bed's been slept in.
TANNER:	(To TOTTY.) Go up and search!
	(TOTTY exits.)
GILDER:	Will you help me get him to the pantry?
	(FERRABY enters.)
FERRABY:	What's the trouble?
TANNER:	Give that man a hand.

95

(FERRABY helps GILDER to take BROOKS off.)

LORD LEBANON comes in wearing pyjamas and dressing-gown.)

LORD LEBANON: I say, did you hear anything? Where's my mother?

TANNER: In her room, I should imagine. What did you hear?

LORD LEBANON: A sort of choking noise.

TANNER: Which is Miss Crane's room?

(FERRABY enters.)

FERRABY: (Quickly) Why?

LORD LEBANON: It's the Old Lord's room.

TANNER: She's not there now.

FERRABY: Where is it?

TANNER: (To FERRABY.) Go up to Totty; go through the whole house. It doesn't matter about waking people up.

(Exit FERRABY running.)

LORD LEBANON: They tried to persuade me to sleep in that room when I came back from India.

TANNER: Who tried to persuade you?

LORD LEBANON: My mother and those two fellows.

(GILDER enters.)

GILDER: Hello, my lord! Did we wake you up?

LORD LEBANON: Somebody did.

TANNER: (To GILDER.) Where's Miss Crane?

GILDER: (Turning up to TANNER.) I haven't the least idea. She walks in her sleep, you know.

96

TANNER: Well, just walk after her and bring her back. Report to those two officers.

GILDER: (Glancing at LORD LEBANON.) I don't think I——

TANNER: Do as you're told!

GILDER: Oh! All right!

(Exit GILDER.)

LORD LEBANON: Good Lord! I wish I could talk to him like that!

TANNER: It's very easy when you've had a little practice.

LORD LEBANON: Do sit down, won't you? You make me nervous standing up. Somebody else was attacked to-night, weren't they?

(Throughout the scene LORD LEBANON talks earnestly and sanely without raising his voice.)

TANNER: I believe so.

LORD LEBANON: I know. I wish it didn't happen. You know, Brooks wasn't a bad fellow.

TANNER: Oh, he's not dead.

LORD LEBANON: But he? Oh, I'm so glad. (Leaning across the table to TANNER-earnestly.) Don't you think it's about time this line was wiped out?

TANNER: This line—I don't understand what you mean.

LORD LEBANON: This sort of thing has been happening for God knows how many years. You ask my mother. (Sitting back.) She's got all their dates, all their names, all their damned pedigrees, all their party per fess and their saltires and trassures. The Lebanons

97

LORD LEBANON:
(Contd)

have always been like that. Didn't you know? (Leaning on table again.) My father was like that. He was fifteen years in the Old Lord's room. (Laughing) mad as a damned hatter!

TANNER:

Yes, I guessed that.

LORD LEBANON:

(Leaning on one elbow.) But he never strangled anybody. (Confidentially and quickly.) The first time I saw it done was in Poonah—a little fellow slipped up behind a big man and put a cloth over his neck and— (Leans back in chair.) By God, he was dead! Fascinating! I tried it on a girl—(Leaning forward.) An Indian girl. She went out like that! (Snaps his fingers.) Extra-ordinary, isn't it?

TANNER:

Yes. very.

LORD LEBANON:

(Taking a scarf out of his pocket.) I've got dozens of these—I brought them back from India. (Lays scarf on table.) I'm not a big fellow, but I'm terribly strong. Feel my arm.

(TANNER feels his arm.)

It's rather a joke! People would never dream it about me. Eh? (Laughing) Of course, they made an awful fuss about this Indian girl, they didn't realize I had the strength to do it. It was a tremendous surprise to them. These babu people had to be squared and Mother sent Amersham to bring me home. He was an awful type of man — a dreadful outsider! A man who'd sign other people's names to cheques— ghastly, isn't it? Don't you have anything to do with him—— You know those two fellows, they used to look after my father. Of course, they're not real footmen——

TANNER:

Yes, I guessed that.

98

LORD LEBANON: ——they're sort of—— Well, they look after me. You understand?

TANNER: Yes, I've understood that.

LORD LEBANON: You know that room my mother wouldn't show you? Well, that's all padded, you know. Rubber cushions all round the walls. I have to go there when I realize things.

TANNER: (Smiling) When you get a little tiresome?

LORD LEBANON: (Shouts at him.) When I realize things! I know what I'm saying! (Calm again.) You know, when I'm quite well I'm mad—I don't realize anything! It's only when I get excited that my brain gets clear.

(TANNER leans over.)

(Sitting back.) Don't touch me!

TANNER: I want a light. Be the pefect host.

LORD LEBANON: I'm awfully sorry. (Lights match and lights TANNER's cigar.) Are you friend or foe?

TANNER: Why, what a question! I'm a friend.

LORD LEBANON: You sent for three doctors to certify me. I heard you on the phone.

TANNER: They were coming to see me.

LORD LEBANON: My mother's been jolly good. She's been administering my father's estate when it should have been under commission— whatever it means—you know more about the law than I do. And she'd have got into awful trouble.

TANNER: Why did you ... Why were you so unkind to Studd?

LORD LEBANON: Studd?

TANNER: The chauffeur.

99

LORD LEBANON: Oh, yes, I'm terribly sorry about that. He was such a good fellow. But I'm afraid of Indians. Some of them tried to kill me— they were very angry about this girl. She was such a stupid girl—a Eurasian or something. Poor old Studd. I didn't know about this beastly ball at the village, and I saw this Indian and I was horribly frightened of him. (Looking round.) I'll show you something. Swear you won't tell anybody?

TANNER: I swear.

LORD LEBANON: (Taking a revolver out of his pocket.) It's the first one I've ever been able to get. I took it out of Brooks' pocket! (Chuckles) That was rather clever, wasn't it? I've always wanted one. You can't strangle yourself, you know. It's rather difficult and they look so ugly. (Shudders) Sometimes I think that the whole line ought to be wiped out. All their escutcheons, and their shields! The line! The line! God Almighty! Carry on the line! Isn't it ridiculous!

TANNER: Poor old boy.

LORD LEBANON: Who do you mean—me? Why do you say that?

TANNER: Well, I've got a boy about your age. (Flicking ash into tray.)

(LORD LEBANON puts his hand on the gun- relaxes.)

LORD LEBANON: You don't like me, do you? (Looking earnestly at TANNER.)

TANNER: Yes, I do. I'm a very good friend of yours.

LORD LEBANON: No, you're not.

TANNER: I was very nice to you at Scotland Yard.

LORD LEBANON: So you were—of course you were. That was clever of me to go up there, wasn't it? I mean that was the last thing you'd expect.

100

TANNER: Yes, that was a clever stroke.

LORD LEBANON: I wonder where Gilder put her?

TANNER: Who?

LORD LEBANON: Aisla. She was looking awfully like that Indian girl this afternoon. I went behind her and put my arms around her... Didn't you hear her run down the stairs? Of course Gilder was near by. Haven't you noticed the way, when she's about, he's always following me? She gets frightened if he isn't there. She knows. That's why she's frightened. She came downstairs the night I smashed up this place. (Looking round.) I don't remember doing it, but I suppose I must have done it... I nearly got Amersham that night! And last night, when I did get him, she saw me coming back into the house... that rather worried her! I'm terribly strong. You wouldn't think so, would you?

TANNER: Oh yes, I would. The first time I saw you I thought this fellow is pretty hefty.

LORD LEBANON: Did you really? My God, you're smart, aren't you? I say, I've worried them to-night, by not drinking that bromide. (Laughs softly.) There are a lot of ways to getting out of that room of mine. They don't know it, but I do! I've fooled them lots of nights!

TANNER: Yes, I expect you've fooled them pretty often. Well, (Rising) I'm going to bed.

(LORD LEBANON rises as TANNER does so.)

LORD LEBANON: You're not going to bed. You're pretending you're not scared, but you are. I frighten people.

TANNER: Well, I'm not frightened. Be sensible and give me that gun. Why do you want to fool

101

TANNER:(Contd) about with a thing like that?

LORD LEBANON: There are lots of things I could do with this.

(Enter LADY LEBANON.)

I could end the line with this?

LADY LEBANON: (LORD LEBANON moves away from her.) Willie! What are you doing? You foolish boy! Give me that pistol!

LORD LEBANON: No, I won't! I have always wanted a pistol—I've asked you dozens of times.

LADY LEBANON: Put it away.

LORD LEBANON: (His back to TANNER.) I've told him— I've told him everything!

(TOTTY enters.)

LADY LEBANON: Put it away.

LORD LEBANON: No——no——

(TANNER and TOTTY make a dive at LORD LEBANON. They struggle. LADY LEBANON stands by the desk, very rigid. LORD LEBANON wrenches himself free. There is a shot. He drops.

Enter GILDER. LADY LEBANON does not move. TANNER and TOTTY make an examination in silence.

FERRABY and AISLA enter. They stop at the sight of the group. AISLA sinks down on sofa.)

LADY LEBANON: Well?

TANNER: (Standing up.) He's dead! My God! What a tragedy!

(All remain silent and quite still.)

102

LADY LEBANON: Dead! Ten centuries of Lebanons and no
one left to carry on the name. A thousand
years of being great— gone out like a
candle in the wind.

(With a bitter — rather hysterical laugh —
she turns, and walks slowly and unsteadily
away.)

SLOW CURTAIN